CONTENTS

DEDICATION

Insert dedication text here. Insert dedication text here. Insert dedication text here. Insert dedication text here. Insert dedication text here. Insert dedication text here. Insert dedication text here. Insert dedication text here. Insert dedication text here. Insert dedication text here.

CONTENTS

ACKNOWLEDGMENTS

Insert acknowledgments text here. Insert acknowledgments text here. Insert acknowledgments text here. Insert acknowledgments text here. Insert acknowledgments text here. Insert acknowledgments text here. Insert acknowledgments text here. Insert acknowledgments text here. Insert acknowledgments text here. Insert acknowledgments text here. Insert acknowledgments text here.

1 SKIDMORE MISSOURI MURDERS

Lonely, lonely, unlucky - just a few words that describe Skidmore, Missouri. The photograph depicts a town that may have been a picture of a typical "small town America" in the past, but even if the image existed, it is gone now.

Today, residents drive trucks to church or gas stations, almost through empty roads and destinations. Good Time Charlies is one of Skidmore's few restaurants and boasts a traditional American menu, but it looks pretty good. Tenderloin seems to be their specialty.

From the beginning of the 20th century to the present, Skidmore's population has declined by half. In search of opportunities available in large cities such as Omaha in the north and Kansas City in the south, residents began to be freed from small, quiet rural areas where there were few opportunities to thrive.

As of 2016, Skidmore still has about 270 people living there, mainly from farming and work at nearby factories.

The work of 23-year-old Bobby Joe Stinet was more fun than the average Skidmore resident. She and her husband, Zeb, bred rat terrier dogs from their homes. To supplement their income, they also worked at the Kawasaki Motors Manufacturing Company in the nearby Maryville.

The couple had been married for about a year. As of December 2004, Bobbie Jo had her first child pregnant for eight months.

"Latter Chatter"
As part of her dog breeding business, Bobby Joe regularly contributed to the forum with a group of fellow rat terrier breeders. The name of the forum

was "Ratta Chatter", and the members discussed how to raise, exhibit and care for dogs.

Bobby Joe was known among other members of the group for her sweet and caring nature. The members discussed their passion for rat terriers and shared details of their lives other than dog rearing. Bobby Joe announced to the group that she was pregnant and was expecting her new arrival in January 2005.

Lisa Montgomery, another breeder and dog show participant from Melburn, Kansas, also announced her pregnancy on the site. Lisa posted that she was pregnant with twins, one died and that she was expecting to give birth to a surviving baby in December. Looking at her pictures at the dog show, fellow breeders had doubts about Lisa's pregnancy claims.

But Bobby Joe had no reason to distrust Lisa. They exchanged messages about the ups and downs of pregnancy, the baby's name and the supplies they plan to buy. In April 2004, Bobby Joe and Lisa met at a dog show in Abilene, Kansas. Everything looked fine.

In late 2004, Jason Dawson received an email from a woman named Darlene Fischer. Dawson was a breeder of rat terriers whom I met at a dog show and a friend of Bobby Joe. He was also a member of Rutter Chatter, whom he met Lisa Montgomery. Dawson had never met Darreen Fisher before, but it was not uncommon to receive emails from strangers asking about puppy adoption.

Fisher asked Dawson if he knew anyone in northern Missouri who had a puppy for adoption because he wanted to buy a puppy for christmas. Dawson knew bobby joe's had been giving birth to garbage recently, and the puppy would be ready to go to the new house in time for Christmas. He told Fisher Bobby Joe's name and her website address www.happyhavenfarms.com.

Fisher emailed Bobby Joe and contacted her via the Chatter Chatter's message board. Her username on the forum was Fischer4kids, which she told a member of a group in Fairfax, Missouri, about a 25-minute drive from Skidmore.

The message from Fisher to Bobby Joe on December 15, 2004 is as follows:

"I was recommended by Jason Dawson, but I couldn't contact him by phone or email. We are considering buying a puppy and will ask you a few questions, so please contact us immediately. ⌐

Bobbie Jo replied to Fisher late that night. She wrote:

"Darren, I emailed you directions so that we could meet. I hope you will receive an email. It's great to chat with you on Messenger. I'm looking forward to chatting with you tomorrow morning. Thank you, Darlene! Have a great night. Bobby. ⌐

December 16, 2004
Zeb Stinnett worked for Kawasaki Motors that day, leaving Bobbie Jo home with his dog and waiting for Darlene Fischer to arrive. Bobbie Jo didn't feel anything different. Fisher met to be completely friendly when they talked at the forum the night before.

Around 2:15 p.m., Bobby Joe spoke with her mother, Becky Harper, on the phone and talked about a woman who came to see the puppy. Bobby Joe, who heard a knock on the door around 2:30 p.m., told his mother that he had to go as the visitor arrived. This is the last time Harper will talk to her daughter.

Bobby Joe answered the door of lisa Montgomery, a familiar woman. But before she could invite her inside, Montgomery intervened and overwhelmed bobby Joe, who was badly pregnant. Lisa made the cord, wrapped it around Bobby Joe's neck, and started squeezing her head from behind until she stopped struggling.

Lisa pushed Bobby Joe back and cut open the uterus with a kitchen knife. When the cut was big enough, she removed the fetus. Wrapped the toddler in a blanket that turned out to be a girl, Lisa went back to the car and drove the car.

Horrible discovery
At 3:30 p.m., Becky Harper came to his daughter. She went into the house and found a scene that could only be explained in a horror movie. Blood was everywhere. Bobby Joe was unconsciously lying on the ground. She clenched a bunch of long blonde hair with her fist.

Harper ran up to the phone and dialed 911. She explained to the operator that her daughter's stomach appeared to have "exploded." There was no sign of an infant anywhere.

The emergency personnel arrived almost immediately, but they were unable to revive Bobby Joe. She was declared dead at 4:27 p.m.

It was concluded that the infant was carried almost to maturity, but probably because it was small, it was likely to be alive. After enduring such a violent birth, the baby may feel pain.

An investigation into who killed Bobby Joe and kidnapped her baby began soon. The authorities knocked on the door and asked the neighbor if they had ever seen anything suspicious that afternoon. A resident said he saw a dirty old red car parked on the driveway of Stinnett around 2:30 p.m. They have never seen a car before.

Nodaway County Sheriff Ben Espey has decided to issue an amber alert to the missing baby. Given that little was known about the baby, it was difficult at first to convince his colleagues of this. Usually you need information about the most basic details, such as eye and hair color, but they didn't. However, an alert was delivered around 12:30 a.m. on December 17.

The next day, as the sun rose, the news of a young mother who had literally killed a baby pulled from the womb spread like a wildfire.

Dyanne Siktar, a North Carolina rat terrier breeder, saw the news that morning and recognized the young pregnant woman as Bobbie Jo Stinnett, a fellow breeder in Missouri. Sitker was shocked and saddened by the murder. She began to think of Bobby Joe as a friend and had many conversations with her at Latter Chatter.

Sitkar has logged on to the forum. Of course, Bobby Joe's tragic murder was in everyone's mind. As he scrolled through the posts over the past two days, Sitoker looked for clues on the message board about what happened to Bobby Joe. She read before and after the trip between Bobby Joe and Darreen Fisher on December 15, where Bobby Joe emailed Fisher about his address and how to get to her house. Fisher was to meet Bobby Joe at home on the 16th. Sitkar looked up Fischer's account name, "fischer4kids." It felt creepy at her. She called the FBI and informed them of her discovery.

Fbi agents began receiving Bobby Joe's emails on December 15. Sure enough, there was an email from Darline Fisher in my inbox. Their attempt to track down women with this name in Fairfax, Missouri, was in vain. Darlene Fisher didn't seem to exist.

The FBI used computer forensic analysis to track the source of emails from Darline Fisher. Led them to a modem connected to a telephone line at Kevin Montgomery's house on South Adams Road in Melvern, Kansas.

Our New Baby
On December 17, Lisa and Kevin Montgomery added a baby girl named Abigail to their families at whistle stop café in Melburn. Lisa told a friend that she was working at a store when she was shopping in Toyca, Kansas the day before.

She was taken to Topeka's Birth Women's Center, where she gave birth to a baby girl. Montgomery called her husband and told him what had happened and that he needed to pick her up.

Kevin and his two teenage children got in his truck, drove to Topeka to pick up Lisa and her new baby.

The couple's friends and family said the baby was small, but otherwise it looked healthy. They did not know the terrible ordeal that the baby had endured now.

Arrest
Meanwhile, FBI agents were waiting for the arrival of an old red car on South Adams Road in Melburn outside a farm in Montgomery. Eventually, the dirty red Toyota Corolla was pulled up, revealing a man and a woman holding a newborn baby.

The agent approached the couple and asked if they were Kevin and Lisa Montgomery. They confirmed it was. Kevin and Lisa went in and the agent followed, asking questions about the baby. Lisa told the same story she was talking to a friend. It was not difficult for the agent to find her. When they told them she had a baby at the Maternity Women's Center in Topeka, agents told her that they had confirmed with the staff there and that she had no record of the baby she had the day before. Lisa Montgomery confessed to have gone bankrupt, strangled and killed her baby's mother, cut her from the womb and kidnapped her.

Kevin Montgomery was shocked by his wife's confession, believing that Lisa was really pregnant.

Lisa was arrested and charged with being killed in an abduction. Kevin was not involved in the killing of Bobby Joe Snett or the abduction of babies, and was found not to have been charged.

During her trial, Lisa Montgomery's longstanding lies and deception were revealed.

Testified were Lisa's ex-husband Carl Bowman, Kevin Montgomery, Kevin Montgomery's ex-wife Lori Colwell, and Jason Dawson, who originally introduced Lisa to Bobby Joe, who she called Darren Fisher.

Bowman, who had detained four children at the time of Lisa's killing, testified that his ex-wife was unable to conceive because of a fallopian suit in 1990 after the birth of the fourth child. Her doctor recommended this procedure because of his belief that Lisa would not be able to carry another pregnancy to term after the child was born two months preterm.

But after her procedure, Lisa forged five more pregnancies while still married to Bowman. Hearing of custody, the day before Bobby Joe's killing, Lisa called him and referred to him, saying she "he was going to prove he was wrong."

Immediately after Lisa was arrested, Bowman told reporters:

Kevin Montgomery testified that his wife claimed to have been pregnant three times since he got married. Every time he believed in her. The first two supposed pregnancies of their marriage ended with Lisa telling Kevin that she had something wrong with her unborn child and she had to have an abortion. But unlike the third time, when he saw Lisa carrying an infant while collecting her in Topeka, he believed it was really his baby.

One of Lisa's relatives told Kevin that Lisa could not get pregnant because she had a tube tied, but Kevin said she did not know what this meant. Kevin's ex-wife, Lori Colwell, testified that she believed Lisa was tricking Kevin into believing she was pregnant. She explained that Kevin had no social skills and was manipulated very easily.

In Lisa's defense
Lisa Montgomery pledged acquittal for the kidnapping leading to the murder. Her lawyer, Fred Duchardt, has decided to pursue crazy defense to avoid the death penalty for his clients.

Duchardt alleged that Lisa experienced a life of mental illness due to the relentless sexual abuse and beating that she received as a child in the hands of her stepfather and mother. From a young age she began to rely on alcohol to relieve pain.

Duchardt also claims that the client suffers from the paranoid pseudocystic disease, a condition in which a woman's body mimics all the signs and symptoms of pregnancy, but does not actually carry the fetus. Did. Famous neuroscientists VD Ramachandran and William Logan MD supported Duchardt's defense as an expert witness during the trial. They confirmed the claim that Lisa was paranoid and probably had pseudocystosis, depression, borderline personality disorder and PTSD.

Federal Prosecutor Rosan Ketchmark and prosecution expert witness Dr. Park Dietz, a forensic psychiatrist, strongly disputed the defense's claims that Lisa has a false sac. Ketchmark argued that the defense against linking murder and abduction to a false sac was a sort of "voodoo science."

Ketchmark does not deny the fact that Lisa suffered this terrible abuse in her infancy, but was deliberately planned because the killing of Bobby Joe Snett was carefully planned by Lisa Montgomery. Insisted. Ketchmark speculated that Lisa was abducting her baby because Lisa worried that her ex-husband would use her fake pregnancy claims against her in custody hearings.

On October 22, 2007, after just five hours of deliberation, a jury pleaded guilty to Lisa for kidnapping. Four days later, they advised her to be sentenced to death. On April 4, 2008, Judge Gary A. Fenner of the US District Court officially sentenced Lisa to death.

51-year-old Lisa Montgomery is a prisoner at the Federal Medical Center in Carswell, Fort Worth, Texas. She is one of the only three women to be executed in the federal system.

Victoria Joe Snett

When Lisa Montgomery confessed to killing Bobby Joe and kidnapping her baby, authorities took her to a hospital in Topeka, where she reunited with her father. Zeb Stinnett called her a "miracle" and named her Victoria Victoria. After a short stay at the hospital, Zeb was allowed to take Victoria Joe home. Despite the trauma she experienced with Lisa Montgomery, she was doing very well.

On the terrifying day of December 2004, Bobby Joe Stinet's family was robbed of his beloved daughter, wife, and sister. "Bobby Joe would have been a wonderful mother," Bobby Joe's mother, Becky Harper, wept.

Bobby Joe wakes up to take a break at Hillcrest Cemetery in Skidmore. Despite the severe cold, more than 400 mourners attended the memorial service. Recalling the tender hearted young woman whose dog walked through the streets of a small town and waved with a smile, they sobbed and hugged each other. The day Bobby Joe was torn from this earth, Skidmore lost one of the few lights that were still there.

Skidmore, Missouri, has seen more violence and wickedness than the average small American village. I'm not talking about murder, but I'm not ominous or ominous.

On April 11, 2001, 20-year-old Branson Kane Perry disappeared in a thin air from outside Skidmore's home. Three years later, his cousin, Bobby Joe Stinet, is killed and an eight-month fetus is excised from the womb and kidnapped. Last year, one of Branson's cousins, Wendy Gillenwater, was beaten to death by his boyfriend.

Here we say that these cases are irrelevant. They wonder to us that a small town could be exposed to so many tragedy... or is there something beyond human understanding at Skidmore? ?

Missing person profile

Height: 5" 9

Weight: 155 pounds

Clothing/Jewelry Description: Size 32 shorts, medium to large T-shirts, necklaces, small leather items, or chains with arrowheads.

Pathology-Heart disease state (tachycardia) allergic to penicillin

Characteristic Features-Caucasian man, very short blonde hair, blue eyes, small faint scar on top of right cheek, small scar on left knee. Perry's wisdom tooth has been removed and there are some fillings on his other teeth. He is right handed

Who is Branson Perry?
Branson Perry was born on February 24, 1981 in Rebecca (Becky) Clino and Bob Perry. In November 2001, Rebecca and Bob divorced. Rebecca moved to another town about 20 miles away from her family's home on 304 West Oak Street in Skidmore, but Branson stayed with her father in a family home.

In 1999, Branson graduated from Nodaway Holt High School. He started a strange job. First a roofer, then a petting zoo. His hobbies were weightlifting and martial arts, specifically Hopkid, where he had a black belt.

In April 2001, 20-year-old Branson was unemployed and lived with his father.

The day Branson disappeared
The information I gathered on Wednesday, April 11, 2001, was in writing from Becky Klino, Branson's mother, and is here.

Bob Perry was hospitalized on the day and came home on Friday, April 13. Branson plans to clean the house in preparation for his father's return, and turned to his friend Jenna Crawford for help. There were two men working outside Bob's car at Branson's home and needed an alternator replacement.

Becky emphasized that the events of the day were not entirely clear to her. I think Gena originally reported this information to the police, perhaps directly to her.

Jenna and Branson were in the middle of cleaning when Branson suddenly went to the kitchen and took something out of the cabinet. When he returned, he didn't tell Gina what he took from the cabinet and why he got out.

Gina took a shower when they finished cleaning. When coming out of the bathroom, she saw one of the men working outside the car pass through the kitchen cabinets (I'm not sure if Branson knew he was at home)). Jenna asked the man what he was looking for. He told her that it was nothing and went outside.

At 3 pm, when I heard the door close, Jenna was on the second floor. She looked out the window on the second floor and saw Branson down the stairs at the front door. She asked him what he was doing and replied that he was going to put the jumper cable in a vault (next to the house) and he would be back soon. This was the last time everyone met Branson Perry.

Gina waited a little more for Branson to return, but he didn't, so she left. I think it's a bit strange that she didn't look for him. Bob had to be hospitalized for another two days, so his mother, Branson's grandmother, Joe Anstinet, went home on Friday to meet Branson. All doors were unlocked, the radio was on, but Branson was not found anywhere. She thought this was strange, but thought he was probably just out, so she left and came back the next day.

Everything was exactly the same as the day before and there were no signs of Branson yet. A little worried at this time, she began calling his friends, but no one saw or heard from him. On Sunday, Joe Ann called Bob and then Becky and told them Branson was missing. Bob left the hospital on Monday and went to see Joan and Becky at the police station. A report of the missing person was submitted to Branson on Tuesday, which had not been seen for six days.

Bob returned home and began to find out if Branson was out of possession, but everything was there, including his wallet and a van that he normally drove. Authorities searched the jumper cable vault, but there were no signs of them. Two weeks later, they strangely appeared in the hut behind the door.

Investigation
Once Perry's property was searched, the Nodaway Country Sheriff

department and public search began to explore areas within a 15-mile radius of the house. Abandoned buildings, farms and fields in the area were thoroughly investigated, but nothing was found. The fact that Branson had been missing for six days before the search began in earnest was a serious setback for the detectives.

Six weeks after disappearance, police interviewed more than 100 people. The claim that I find really strange is that the two men who worked outside Bob's car on the day of disappearance said they had seen nothing. Surely if Branson had just left, would they have met him? Or if it was attacked and thrown into a car, couldn't it be missed? I think they are hiding something.

Gina was interrogated and admitted that she and Branson were experimenting with drugs such as marijuana and methamphetamine. The detectives therefore attributed Branson's disappearance to drug-related and possibly fraudulent activity.

Authorities were able to track an acquaintance of the Branson family in nearby St. Joseph, Missouri. Some were given the lie detector test, they all passed. They could not determine that Branson owed money to the drug dealer. Given the secrets associated with these people, I hope the detectives have not progressed without taking their words as they are. Unfortunately, drug-motivated murders are always much harder to resolve.

The two main suspects who appear in this case over and over again are Jason Bierman, a neighbor next to Branson (some sources spell only one'n'), 59 It is Jack Wayne Rogers, an all-year-old Presbyterian Minister. Vulgar human.

Jason Beerman
Most of the information I've found on Jason reported here is pre-owned information from a book called Baby Be Mine by Diane Fanning, originally focused on Bobbie Jo Stinnett. I couldn't access the book, but I've gotten it many times on Wikipedia and other true crime blogs. There is no coverage of Jason, and I do not know where Fanning found these details about what happened between Jason and Branson.

On April 7, 2001, the day before Branson was missing, he went to Jason's house. I don't know if there was a particular reason he went or if they were going to hang out. I don't know Jason's age, but I did a little search on his name and found that a 49-year-old man lived in Mound City, Missouri (about 25 minutes from Skidmore) under the name Jason Beerman. .. If this is Jason, he is 11 years older than Branson and 31 when Branson disappears.

According to Fanning, Jason administered the drug to Branson when he came. Branson then stripped off all his clothes, danced naked at Jason's house, and shaved his pubic hair. Branson and Jason then "sexed". No one is told that Branson was raped, but it seems suspicious because Branson had been given a drug.

When Branson arrived, he understood what had happened and was completely humiliated. Then Branson apparently went home and told his father what had happened (I found this kind of amazing thing). Bob wasn't surprised to see Branson having sex with another man, because he suspected his son was homosexual for a while, but was frightened by Jason's use of him. I read that Bob was thinking of "teaching Biaman a lesson," but opposed it. Bob didn't want to pay attention to what happened, perhaps because it's a very conservative part of the country where homophobia is endemic. Some people also speculate that Bob, who was in and out of the hospital, was ill and was unable to fight older men.

Bob tells the detective what happened between Branson and Jason on April 7.

Many believe that Jason is responsible for Branson's death. I've seen talks on forums (I'm not sure if this is accurate either). Jason Beerman left Skidmore for two weeks after Branson disappeared. Nobody knew where he went. I couldn't find anything about whether the detective asked him about this. Maybe Jason was worried that something might happen between them, so he killed Branson and drove somewhere far away to fill his body.

Jack Wayne Rogers

Rogers, a Presbyterian minister from Fulton, Missouri, and leader of the Boy Scouts, became a suspect who disappeared when Branson was arrested for possessing child pornography in April 2003. He was also charged with the first assault on a failed attempt at a transsexual surgery (he had no medical qualifications or knowledge) to a trans-woman Madison (born Michael) Abercrombie in a hotel room in Columbia, Missouri. It was. Abercrombie almost died of blood loss and had to call a paramedic.

The detective searched Rogers' computer for child pornography, and found several posts that Rogers picked up a skidmore blonde male hitchhiker, raped, tortured, killed, and buried a man's body in Ozarks.

But when asked about this, Rogers denied it had anything to do with Branson, claiming he didn't know who he was. He claimed the entire account was structured and was just a fantasy. The detective also discovered a tortoise claw necklace in a Rogers car that appeared to belong to Branson.

Rogers was convicted and sentenced to 17 years for assault and seven years for illegal surgery. He was sentenced to 30 years in prison for possessing child pornography. The sentences are executed simultaneously.

Becky Krino attended Rogers' hearing and asked her to tell her what happened to Branson's body. However, he claimed nothing to do with Branson's disappearance. She would later tell the media about Rogers:

"The police haven't eliminated him completely, but now the investigation is again heading to Skidmore. They're taking a new lead there. In time there is a way to unravel the secrets. I think someone in the area knows what happened to Branson, and in my mind I don't think this suspect is responsible. I [in his judgment] Despite the nightmares I have experienced, I am grateful that such an evil person will never walk down the street again."

What was in the cupboard?
Internet detectives/web detectives are very focused on what was in the kitchen cabinets Branson took outside. Most speculate that it was drugs or money. Perhaps, whatever it was, he took him to someone waiting outside. If it was drugs or money, they counted it and found that it was not enough. So they sat in the car waiting for Branson to come out of the house again-they knew Gina was there, so they just didn't want to get stuck. When Branson came out of the house with a jumper cable, they grabbed him, threw him into his car, and got out of the car. I'm inclined to have at least two people. Branson wasn't that big, but he was training and doing martial arts, so he could have defended himself if he was the only one.

Jumper cable
Many people speculate that he was strangled with a jumper cable, but I

think it's likely they just grabbed him and ran away-it takes time to strangle someone, The longer they stay in the property, the more likely someone will have seen them. Branson was holding a jumper cable when he disappeared, so he got in the car with him.

The jumper cable folds back in the storage shed after two weeks is the only reason I can think of. ? As far as I know, jumper cables have not been tested for DNA evidence of any kind.

My thoughts
Much of the information about this case turned out to be very crude in terms of details. Everything was so ambiguous. Obviously, all my research is done online, so I can see why there is a gap in this story.

First of all, I am interested in Jenna Crawford. If she were Branson's good friend, she would have had to agree to clean up with him that day (and take a shower at his house), before she left her Why didn't you look for it? It also sounds like he didn't try to get in touch with him again after Wednesday, but I think she thought so if he left without saying goodbye immediately after he disappeared. I wondered if she had tried to reach him, but when I couldn't reach him, I thought he was probably using drugs with others and just didn't want to get involved. This could also explain why she didn't contact the authorities because she didn't want to get him in trouble.

As mentioned above, I have doubts about the man who was repairing the car and how to claim that they hadn't seen anything. Also very strange is one of those who wanders through the house and through the kitchen cabinets. I also wonder why Gina didn't mention this to Branson. Maybe she did, but I couldn't find anything she did. It would be amazing if a man repairing a car in my house started wandering through the kitchen cabinets (unless they were actually Branson's friends).

According to the Charlie Project, Branson's family and friends said Branson's "not very characteristic" was that he could not be contacted with his friends or family for more than a few days. If so, I just wonder why no one raised the alert before he was missing for six days already.

Since Branson's disappearance
In my opinion, the only way to know what happened to Branson is if

someone came up before. The search happens every year, but nothing happens. There are few hints.

The case is treated as a murder. In April 2019, Nodaway County Sheriff Randy Strong said he had a good idea of who was responsible based on information gathered by former Sheriffs. The same name will still pop up in the case file. It's hard when you have no body, but Strong believes they are closer than ever to see what actually happened to Branson. When he feels they have sufficient evidence to prove their case, it is taken to the Public Prosecutor's Office.

Branson's father, Bob Perry, died in 2004. Becky Clino, dedicated to devoting her life to Branson's disappearance, died tragically in 2011 in melanoma. She was 52 years old. Her son.

After her death, Sergeant Sgt. Roger Phillips, an investigator in the Highway Patrol Drug and Crime Department of the Missouri and Becky's friend, said:

"Just because [Kurino-san] isn't here doesn't mean the train doesn't keep moving. It's about knowing the truth."

Becky was buried near an empty plot that had been dug for Branson. His death is listed on the tombstone on April 11, 2001, the day he disappeared.

The killing of Kenlex McElroy is not "unresolved" in the general sense. It's not like an unsolved murder for decades, and eventually someone suggests a tip to break the case. This is far from what happened with McElroy. In fact, on the hot July day of 1981, between 30 and 90 people were seen shooting a 270 pound man.

Someone saw something.

However, no one is making progress. There was silence between the witnesses. The truth is that the people of Skidmore, Missouri, were tired of tired of living their lives in fear under Ken McKellroy's tyrannical rule of more than 20 years. Someone had to put an end to it. And that's exactly what they did.

Who was Ken Rex McElroy?

Born June 1, 1934 in Overland Park, Kansas, McKellroy was the 15th of Tony and Mabel McKellroy's 16 children. McElroys had no money. They worked as share croppers and moved frequently before settling in Skidmore.

The children had little parental supervision, and most were free running throughout the city. McElroy dropped out in the second year of middle school. He was widely reported to be illiterate, but he did not stop him from getting what he wanted in life.

Shortly after leaving school, McElroy had a head injury when he fell from a hay wagon. He was reportedly so serious he needed to have a steel plate in his head. Many speculate that this trauma was responsible for his instability and aggression.

By his teens, McElroy became known as Skidmore's "town bully." He ruled with an iron fist, fueled fear and caused persistent fear among the townspeople.

Ultimate blackmailer
Upon leaving school (and probably before), McElroy began stealing items such as antiques, alcohol, grains, and gasoline. He was often found hunting raccoon dogs and was infamous for ringing pigs and cows in a small agricultural community.

It was not long before he became his more serious crime, including violent threats, rape, attacks and child abuse. As a result, he was no stranger to Nodaway County Sheriff.

To describe McElroy as intimidating is to underestimate it. Every time someone accused him (this happened a total of 21 times), he threatened the indictor withdrawing it, scaring them and scaring their lives.

His preferred methods of intimidation included approaching people, swooting threats, and pushing shotguns into their faces. He also took them home, sat outside of his truck and stared at them with his dark ominous gaze for hours.

Once upon a time, a farmer named Romaine Henry found McKellroy trespassing on his property and tried to get rid of it. Instead of leaving, McElroy turned around and shot Henry into his stomach with his shotgun.

Henry survived and, unlike most of McElroy's other victims, actually continued to testify to him in court. It wasn't enough to be hungry. McElroy was acquitted because of his talented lawyer. Many speculate that McElroy also threatened the jury.

It cannot be denied that McElroy is a skilled criminal. His long-breaking law-breaking career resulted in a pocket permanently packed with $100 bills. But much of his cash was paid to his lawyer, Richard Jean McFaddin. McFadin was a highly skilled lawyer who pulled McElroy over and over again.

It seemed that McElroy had escaped from the law enough to escape. The people of the town resented the constant feelings of anxiety that the presence of McElroy left to them. But even more frustrating was the law enforcement agency's inability to handle the monsters that scared them on a daily basis.

Ken McElroy's many wives
Support yourself. This part is a roller coaster.

McElroy got almost what he wanted, and the woman was no exception. However, most of his sexual problems were not about women, but about minor girls he had at least 10 children in a group.

To my knowledge, McElroy has been married three times. His first wife, Sharon, was 15 years old when he met, while McElroy was at least 20 years old. McElroy wasn't a dear husband, and beat Sharon regularly. Ultimately, Sharon and McElroy had two children. By the time he had a second child, Musselroy found another girlfriend, Sally (age 13), but Ken was 27. McElroy moved Sally to a family farm with Sharon and his two children. Sally had McKellroy and three children, and Sharon had two more.

McElroy quickly bored Sharon, Sally, and his seven children, and found another minor girl, Alice Wood, widely referred to as McElroy's second wife. McElroy left the family home and was with Alice, but the relationship remained the same as it used to be. He verbally and physically abused Alice, and when she gave birth to their son, she lived with her mother and stepfather, from Skidmore to the next town, St. Joseph.

Furious with Alice leaving her son, McCallroy called home and began to threaten Alice and her family. He tells them that he will pick up his son, and if someone tries to stop him, he will kill them. Alice's stepfather, in so many words, told McElroy to push it out. McElroy drove to his house and shot his foot through the living room window.

McElroy was arrested on charges of assault, but Alice's stepfather would have to testify. To stop him from doing so, McElroy continued his usual terrifying tactics-he told him he would kill the whole family if he testified, chasing him and sitting outside the house for hours. After all, Alice's stepfather dropped charges of assault after McElroy threatened with a shotgun after a quarrel at Bar.

After all that had happened between McElroy and her family, Alice returned to McElroy's house with her son. McElroy found another 12-year-old girlfriend, Trena McCloud, to welcome her, but McElroy was 35. At the age of 14, Torena was pregnant. After giving birth, exhausted by the constant fear of McElroy, Trena and Alice left their McElroy farm with their children to live with her parents.

Needless to say, McElroy didn't have any of this. He went to Torena's parents' house, where he severely hit Torena and Alice, and then burned McCloud's house to the ground. He pushed the two women and children into his truck and returned them to the farm.

Torena had to go to the hospital because of an injury injured by McElroy. The doctor who treated her was appalled and called for child service. Torena participated in foster care with her son.

McElroy was charged with arson, rape, and deadly weapon-wielding. However, although his lawyer managed to delay this procedure, Torena, still a child and very naive, got tired of foster care and fled. She returned with her son to a McElroy farm. McElroy divorced from Sharon (or Alice, to be honest, I don't know who he was married to) and married Torena, so she didn't have to testify to him. She dropped the charge.

Ernst "Bo" Bowenkamp
In April 1980, McElroy's two daughters were shopping at a local corner store. An older daughter paid for her goods, but when they left, the next

daughter grabbed the candy from the jar and headed for the door. The clerk saw what happened and warned the girl that she should either return the candy or pay for it. The older girl took the candy from the younger girl, put it back in the jar, grabbed her sister's hand and pushed it out the door.

The clerk didn't think anything further until Ken and Torena McKellroy appeared. Neither was talking about an incident that does not seem to matter. Of course, McElroy had a gun. By this time, Torena, who was 23 years old, started yelling at the clerk, drawing the attention of the clerk Ernst and Lois Bowenkamp. The two came out from behind the store and were also the subject of the couple's anger. Lois got tired quickly and told McKellroy not to leave the store and never come back.

They left, but for McElroy, it wasn't over. Bowencamps became the new target of McElroy's intimidation program. He sat on his truck outside the house for hours in the evening. Several times he got off the truck and fired a shotgun into the air-all this on a piece of candy. Boenkamp, who was in his early 70s at the time, did his best to lead a normal life. But it wasn't easy for this thug with a serious anger problem to breathe his neck 24 hours a day, 7 days a week. Then one day, Musselroy drove to the corner store, found Bo Bowenkamp in the back and shot his neck.

Bo survived and McElroy was arrested...but he was released on bail and began harassing police officer Richard Stratton who arrested him. This lasted for several months as his trials were constantly delayed. McElroy roamed around town as usual, drinking for hours at his usual hangout, D & G Tavern.

For the first time in his life, McElroy was actually convicted of a crime. However, the result of the conviction was the slap faced by Bo and Lois Bowenkamp. His conviction was for two assaults, and he was sentenced to only two years.

Residents of Skidmore were pleased that (some) justice was finally offered. But, of course, McElroy filed an appeal of his belief and was issued on a bond of $40,000 while his appeal was pending. This was the limit of intuition for everyone at Skidmore. The judicial system made them fail again.

For revenge
Upon his release, McElroy walked to the D & G tavern with a bayonet-

mounted rifle. Despite his belief, he was still the arrogant gown he always used to. He wielded a gun in the bar and declared that he would end Bo Bowenkamp. Several patrons witnessed McElroy's display at a tavern and called the prosecutor who canceled McElroy's bail. A hearing is scheduled and witnesses testify that they saw McElroy at the bar holding the loaded weapons.

Then, on July 9, 1981, Richard McFadin postponed the hearing for two weeks. It was at this time that the anger of the locals reached a boiling point. Nearly 50 of them had come together to make a plan to protect the witnesses who were trying to testify against McKellroy. The hearing was postponed and McKellroy knew exactly who the witnesses were, so the whole town felt a pressing sense of destiny over what was to come.

Vigilante justice
The next morning, people gathered again. This time, we gathered at the American Legion Hall opposite D & G Tavern. The plan was to discuss how to protect yourself from McElroy for the next two weeks before the hearing. Authorities disappointed them, so they had no choice but to put the problem in their hands.

While the meeting was taking place, McElroy returned to the D & G tavern drinking with Torena. After the meeting, the group crossed the street to the tavern and confronted McKellroy. I felt a sense of security in numbers.

Forty of them stood outside, but another twenty were flocking to a small tavern. They surrounded McElroy, had enough, and yelled to him that his days were counted.

McElroy and Torena rose without saying a word and pushed through the crowd towards the exit. Groups outside the tavern grew up and began to get angry when they saw the couple come out of the tavern. McElroy and Torena got into the truck. Before driving, McElroy stopped to ignite the cigarette.

Two gunshots rang like he did when he was taking his first drag. The windows of the truck shattered. At least one bullet hit McKellroy behind the head. Blood covered Torena, who was sitting inside the car and in the passenger seat. McElroy plunged forward on the steering wheel.

Someone opened the passenger door and pulled Torena from the truck into another nearby building. She was shocked, but not physically injured.

Nobody called an ambulance. McElroy died on the scene surrounded by people who had been in terror for decades. It would be naive to say they didn't feel collective relief.

Harry McLean, the author of the award-winning book Interviewing the people that were out there that day, about McKellroycase, who spent several years living in Skidmore. From talking to witnesses, he concludes that McKellroy's killing was not planned.

McLean told Inside Edition: I have never felt sorry for him. No one was sick. Someone was about to be killed. It will be him or someone else. "

No investigators confessed or provided information about who shot the deadly shot. Unsurprisingly, the residents of Skidmore were angry at the presence of town police. Why did they enthusiastically carry out this investigation into the killing of a man who has long misered people's lives? One man said to a police officer who was investigating the scene: "What are you doing here? Why are you doing this? You know what he was like. You are him Knows how we oppressed and intimidated us. I don't think you are coming now after I have been in need of your help."

Torena was the only person to go to the detectives about who she believed she had killed her husband. She saw a man named Del Clement, co-owner of D & G Tavern, standing across the street with a rifle. But it was too late. No one else supports the story of Torena. Del Clement later died and he did not confess. It is widely accepted that he fired one of the guns that shot McElroy. Secretly, Skidmore was very grateful to him.

Torena left Skidmore, remarried, and had more children. She died of cancer in 2012 at the age of 55.

Ken Rex McElroy was buried at Memorial Park Cemetery in St. Joseph, Missouri. He was 47 years old. His gravestone has the words "brave, fearless, compassionate." I feel that his neighbor would have described him somewhat differently.

2 THE DELPHI MURDERS

Before investigating and writing about this case, I knew virtually nothing, so I started almost from the beginning. Only two years have passed since the bodies of Abbey and Libby were discovered on February 14, 2017 in their hometown of Delphi, Indiana. No one was found guilty of the brutal killing of two girls, and officials have published relatively little information.

The lack of certain facts about the incident created a rumor and a hotbed of rumor that stretches its legs. It can be difficult to tell what is fact and what is fiction.

The truth is that rumors can do harm and hinder investigation. They can cause more pain and hurt to a family who is sad about their loved one. For these reasons, I will not accept these rumors here.

Since we published this post, there have been updates regarding the survey. You can read my post about updates here.

Abigail (Abby) Williams and Liberty (Libby) German

Abby's mother, Anna and her grandparents, and Libby's grandparents, Mike and Becky Patty, and her sister, Kelshi, have worked with investigators in all ways to help keep the case alive. They are speaking at a press conference and aren't hesitating from the media to keep the case openly hidden. While they wait for justice for the girls, I am completely in awe of their power and grace during this unimaginable and difficult time.

In 2018, a family of both girls joined CrimeCon in Nashville. There, Indiana Police officers Anna, Mike, Becky, and Sergeant Jerry Hallman attended a murder-and-quest session on murder with host Ashley Banfield. Libby's sister, Kelsi, had her mission to seek justice for Abby and Libby. She can be found on Twitter, here, on her Instagram here.

Abbey and Libby were close friends and spent endless hours together inside and outside the school. They were together in a school band, loved exploring the outdoors and taking pictures, and planned to start softball together at school.

Libby was thoughtful, affectionate, generous and sociable. She loved sports, especially swimming, living outdoors, painting and baking. Her ambition was to become a science teacher or crime scene investigator, and she even attended additional science classes outside of Purdue University's school.

According to her mother, Anna, Abby was always laughing. She was caring, selfless, funny and loved to be with friends and family. Abby was creative. She loved art and photography and loved making gifts for people. Abbey played volleyball at school and enjoyed going out on a camping trip with her family.

The Abbey and Libby Celebration of Life is an annual event, with the final event taking place on September 29, 2018. All proceeds from the event were donated to the Abbey and Libby Memorial Park Foundation. The park is still under construction and is actively accepting donations to drive the process. Learn more about.

February 13-15, 2017
February 13
Indiana was a warm day in February. Liberty German (14) and Abigail Williams (13) attended the Delphi Community Middle School. Delphi is a very small city with less than 3000 people in Carroll County, Indiana.

The two girls decided to spend the afternoon enjoying the weather and exploring the Delphi Historic Trail. Around 1:35 pm, Libby's sister, Kelsi, dropped them off on the trail head of the Monon High Bridge Trail. Nothing seemed crazy until another family arrived that afternoon to pick up girls at a set time and place and no one was there. It soon became clear that something was wrong. The girl's family searched the area for a few hours and found nothing. At 5:30 pm, Abbey and Libby were reported missing.

Carroll County Sheriff, headed by Sheriff Torbery Zenby, Delphi Police, Delphi Fire Department, and the general public all participated in the search for two girls. At 11:45 pm, the search was suspended due to darkness, but was resumed the next morning.

February 14
At 12:45 pm on February 14, two bodies were discovered by members of the fire department and civilians near Deer Creek, about 0.5 miles east of Monon High Bridge. The fire chief reported the survey results as "bad". The media was informed about the discovery, but not the identity of the body.

February 15
Necropsy was performed and confirmed to be that of Abbey Williams and Libby German. It was also confirmed that the girls were killed.

To date, we do not know the cause of death and the autopsy report is sealed.

Evidence-what do we know?
The girl was killed at 2:07 pm. This time is when Libby walked Anon's Snapchat over the Monn High Bridge. I was killed (or taken somewhere) before my family came to pick me up (I read around 3:15).

Two pieces of evidence that highlighted this case are a photo and voice recording of a man Libby recorded on the phone. She recorded a video of a man actually walking, but only a still image from the video was released. The photo shows a white man looking down while crossing a bridge. He puts his hands in his pockets and wears jeans, a dark blue jacket, and a hat that looks like flaps on his ears.

Initially, the investigators said they only wanted to talk to the guy in the photo. But a few days later, it was officially announced that he was a suspect.

The voice is the voice of a man saying, "Down the hill." There is more audio, but investigators haven't released it. Audio is described as muffled. It has been suggested that Libby may have recorded the man with his cell phone in his pocket. You can listen here.

Just a week after the girl was found murdered, 46 states displayed 6000 bulletin boards with expanded versions of photos Libby took of a man on a bridge. By March 9, the reward for information leading to the arrest of the suspect had risen to $240,000.

The body was found at the edge of Ronald Logan's 77-year-old property. Logan was a habitual traffic offender, with multiple DUIs. At the time of the killing, he was released on parole for these crimes. In the murder afternoon, he drove to the county litter dump and saw him drink at the Pizza King restaurant for several hours. Investigators proved that Logan was not involved in the murder, but he was imprisoned in April 2017 for violating parole.

On July 17, 2012, Indiana Police released a sketch (below) of a man on the bridge. He is a 5'6" to 5'10" Caucasian man weighing 180-220 pounds with auburn hair. There are various reports, but I expect 40 to 55 years old.

Unfortunately, this has been posted on the forums by placing it next to individuals whose sketches look similar as a result of the proliferation of internet detectives. As mentioned earlier, this is useless for investigation and can seriously undermine the reputation of an innocent individual.

What do we not know?
A lot. There is no doubt that we know much more than investigators allow. Evidence should be placed near the chest so that when the suspect is found, he can be asked to know only the answer, for example regarding a specific injury to the body.

If evidence of DNA is found in the field.

When a girl is sexually assaulted.

How Abbey and Libby died.

"New Evidence" Found in First Half of January 2019: Carol County Sheriff Torbery Zenby smashed rumors of new evidence. They continue to analyze with the evidence they already have for something they may have missed.

Daniel Nations
Once upon a time, 31-year-old Daniel Nations was considered an "interested person" in the Delphi murder case. In September 2017, Nations were arrested on Mount Herman, Colorado for threatening a hiker with a hatchet. He was found guilty in December 2017 and received three years of supervised probation and the possibility of prison if he violated the terms of

his probation.

In February 2018, a Johnson County delegate in Indiana traveled to Colorado to retrieve Nations and put him in county jail for being charged with being unable to register as a sex offender in Indiana. Detectors of the Delphi murder case received many tips on the similarities between Nations' Magshot and a sketch of the man on the bridge in Delphi. He was also said to be living homeless in Morgan County, Indiana when Abbey and Libby's bodies were discovered.

However, in mid-February 2018, investigators announced that Nations was not the suspect in the Delphi murder case.

Just a rumor
He believes 46-year-old Charles Eldridge, who was arrested in January 2019 for a sex offense against children in Randolph County, Indiana (more than 100 miles from Delphi), could be a Delphi murderer. Rumors have begun. While Eldridge is arguably a vulgar man to be confined, there was nothing to tie him to the Delphi murder other than the fact that it was somewhat similar to Delphi's sketches.

The Randolph County Sheriff replied to the public in an open letter:

"Except for the sketch-like person, there is currently zero evidence linking him to the [Delphi] case, and he is not a suspect."

Following this, they also said:

"I understand that people are trying to help the investigation, but doing this without evidence other than just appearance can hurt or hinder the investigation."

My thoughts on murder
A bit of my detective job, it may be completely wrong. If you're not interested in any kind of guessing, skip this part!

I personally don't think the suspect is from Delphi – in less than 3000 cities people know each other and can identify a man on the bridge from his appearance and voice. I can do it.

So I think he killed the girl and left the area shortly thereafter. There are a lot of people looking for Abbey and Libby, so if he stayed in the area, someone would have seen him. The photos didn't go live until a few days later, but you probably remembered seeing a man in a coat with a hat on (unless you took off your jacket and put it in your search?).

I think it's an opportunity crime. I don't think he planned it. I think Abby and Libby were terribly unlucky because they were in the wrong place at the wrong time and faced a very evil man. Assuming he wasn't from Delphi, he wouldn't know the girls would leave school Monday afternoon. Maybe he saw them fall out and chase them, but I think it was the scope of any plan he had made.

We don't know the details of how the girl was killed-if he used a knife, a gun, another weapon or his hand. I think he might have hidden some sort of weapon under the coat. But I don't want to guess any more.

Also, I don't know what else happened to the audio Libby recorded. The main reason officials released this short clip was probably because they wanted to see if someone could recognize the voice. So it's so short that it's difficult to know the context. Since their bodies were found at the foot of the hill near Dire Creek, I tend to say it "down the hill" is a command to the girls. Other audio may contain some threat, but it has not been confirmed yet.

The audio recording was probably done on a pretty bad bridge. It's not a bridge you can come across if you need to escape from someone.

what we can do
Those who closely track this case, and/or those who are interested in a real crime, will probably not find new information here. If you don't know this case at all, I hope you read this and know a little more.

The most important thing right now is for people to keep talking about this case over time. The more it remains in the minds of people, the more likely investigators will receive the necessary tips to decipher the case.

On the second anniversary of the murder, Carol County prosecutor Nicholas McClellan stressed that the case was not cool. Police have received more than 38,000 tips since the girls were killed. At the moment, we receive at least 12 tips per day.

If you live in or near the area and have any information that you think might be useful, call the police and call it, even if you think it's just the smallest detail. It may just be the tip they need, you never know.

Indiana Police believe Abbey and Libby murderer "hiding in front of you"

Press conference supervisor Douglas Carter said police were currently looking for drivers for vehicles parked in DCS offices in Delphi, and later on Carroll County Road 300 North between noon and 5 pm. Said it was found near Hoosier Heartland. highway. No further details have been announced, except where the vehicle was parked. I don't know the color, make/model or license number.

More audio has been released. This extends the suspect's original voice and says "go down the hill." The voice was recorded on Libby's mobile phone. The new words sound like "Guys", "down the Hill", but the audio quality is not the best.

A video of "A man in the bridge" walking on the bridge has also been released. Supt. Carter urged the public to pay close attention to his attitude while he was walking. There is a large gap between the slats that make up the abandoned Monong Takahashi, so he looks down when walking.

The most important new information is the updated sketch. Supt. Carter said of the suspect:

"Also, this person is from Delphi and has lived here or before, and regularly visits or works here. This person is in the 18 to 40 age group. But it may look younger than it actually is."

The new sketch figures are now their main suspects. The previous sketch is a by-product of the new sketch.

3 THE DISAPPEARANCE OF BRIAN SHAFFER

If there was a case in favor of the alien abduction, it would have been Brian Scheffer's case. At one point, I was surrounded by people in a crowded bar in downtown Columbus, Ohio. Next time he is gone and I haven't seen or heard him ever since. As of April 1, 2019, Bryan will be missing for 13 years.

Brian is described as 6 feet 2 inches tall, caucasian, approximately 165 pounds, with brown hair and hazel eyes. There is a black spot on his left iris.

When he disappeared, he wore an olive green short-sleeved polo shirt over a white long-sleeved shirt, blue jeans, white adidas sneakers, and a yellow rubber gun awareness bracelet.

He is currently classified as a missing endangered species. At the end of this work, you can see the poster of Brian's missing person.

Brian sheffer
Brian Randall Scheffer was born on February 25, 1979 and grew up in the suburbs of Columbus, Pickering. His parents were Randy and Lenny, and he had his brother Derek.

When she disappeared in 2006, Brian was 27 years old, a second year medical student at Ohio State University, and had a previous bachelor's degree in microbiology.

In early March 2006, Brian's mother died of a rare form of bone cancer. According to his friends, Brian seemed to handle his mother's death fairly well, but thought they might find it more difficult to deal with than he forgave.

Brian was an avid musician and his instrument of choice was the guitar.

His favorite band was Pearl Jam, who even had a tattoo on the cover art of the single Alive band on his right upper arm. Brian was also a fan of Jimmy Buffet. He played music in the same genre as Buffet and aimed to lead a similar relaxed lifestyle. He joked with friends that his medical career was a back-up plan to the real ambition that he was a musician.

At OSU, Brian met the medical student Alexis Wagoner and started dating. They were with Brian for about a year at the time of his disappearance. The two were planning to head to Miami during the spring break of 2006.

The night of March 31, 2006
It was the beginning of Friday and spring break. Brian was ready to relax. He had just finished a stressful week of exams and woke up late to study. In addition to this, he was still dealing with the mother's recent death.

Brian's father, Randy, came to Columbus that evening, had a great time with his son, and took him to dinner. The two went out to a steak restaurant. At dinner, Randy noticed Brian's tiredness and felt he shouldn't go out drinking with friends that night. But he didn't say anything because he knew Brian was an adult and he could make these choices himself.

Brian said goodbye to Randy, headed for the ugly Tuna Saruna, where he met his friend William "Clint" Florence at about 9:30 pm. From there, Clint and Bryan flew around the bar, taking shots everywhere they went and heading down the high street to the Arena District.

Side Note: Ugly Tuna Salona and Surrounds
The ugly tuna was on the second floor of the South Campus Gateway Complex, just south of the OSU campus. The area surrounding the Gateway Complex is always busy with students, especially on Friday nights.

True Crime Garage hosts Nick and Captain from Columbus shared their impressions of the OSU campus area in 2006. The campus was in the process of being "cleaned up" at the time to encourage more students. Apply and attend university. A new modern business has taken the place of a little older bar and restaurant. It was dirty at the time, not particularly clean and not particularly safe. However, some believe that the "cleanup" of the campus has lost some of its character.

The ugly tuna was a large room with a bar in the middle. At the front entrance, go up the escalator, turn right, and cross the landing/atrium type small space. Anyone who goes in or out of these doors gets caught by surveillance cameras.

The ugly tuna had a bathroom and a doorway for staff. The details of this exit are not really clear. From what I could collect, this exit was leading to the construction site at the time. Some sources call this an emergency exit. Importantly, it was not intended for public use. With this exit, I think you didn't have to visit the construction site. You can enter the site or exit the street.

The construction site is very dangerous and obviously no ordinary people can pass through. This site was no exception. It was reportedly difficult for a calm person to navigate, let alone a drunk person.

Therefore, the only way to leave the ugly tuna is through the front door or an emergency exit leading to the construction site. I also don't know if the surveillance camera was working at this exit. I'm leaning no, but I'm not sure.

The night continued...
Around 10 pm, Brian called Alexis, who was visiting Toledo's family that night, and told her that she loved her and was excited about the trip.

Brian and Clint met Clint's friend Meredith Reed on April 1st at about 12:00 am. She got them back on the ugly tuna, where they saw a live band playing and planned to have their last drink before calling it night.

Around 1:15 AM, Clint, Meredith, and Bryan were recorded by surveillance cameras on an escalator to the entrance to the ugly tuna. From the top of the escalator to the beginning was Brian who seemed to be tipsy (of course) in footage. When they entered the bar, they disappeared outside the camera. There were no surveillance cameras in the bar.

Upon entering the ugly tuna, Brian left Clint and Meredith, but claimed to have seen Brian talking to the band. At 1:55 am, 5 minutes just before the ugly tuna closed at 2:00 am, Brian was recorded on a surveillance camera talking to two college girls. Next, I saw Brian descending from the camera towards the bar entrance. Here's Brian's last official sighting. He has not been seen since then.

Around 2:00 am when Clint and Meredith departed, they called Bryan, but there was no response. The two quickly scanned the bar, then stood outside to see if Brian would appear. They called him again when he had no sign, but there was still no answer. They thought he had left without telling them. At 2:9 am, security footage recorded Clint and Meredith leaving the escalator and going to the parking lot where Meredith's car was parked.

On Saturday morning, Alexis called Bryan, but received only voicemail. She wasn't worried, assuming he was still asleep after a big night out. She kept calling him all day long, but there was no answer. By Sunday, Alexis was afraid to contact Brian's father and let him know he couldn't be reached. She was also worried because they were going to fly to Miami the next day. On Monday, Alexis went to the airport in the hope that Brian was there and they could go on holiday and forget what happened. But Bryan didn't show up at the airport. He was subsequently reported missing.

Search
The investigation began with the ugly tuna where Brian's last official sighting took place. Investigators also searched the surrounding area and trash cans behind the building, but nothing was found.

Tracking dogs were used to find nearby waterways and sewers. Investigators took the dog inside and outside the bar to see if it could pick up the scent, but there was none.

Brian's apartment was 6 blocks from the ugly tuna. The investigator went to his apartment to see if there were any problems and found nothing. Everything was in order and Brian's car was parked in the usual places.

Randy desperately contacted the psychiatrist, and he said Brian's body would be found in the body of water. Randy and Derek, along with Brian's officials, searched Columbus for the Olentangy River, about a mile away from Brian's apartment (see map above). There was no sign of Brian yet.

Investigation
Ugly tuna and band staff were queried for investigators and anyone who might have contacted Bryan that night. The staff and band were supportive but failed to provide useful information about Brian's disappearance.

This makes sense given how busy the bar was that night. There would be no reason to notice Brian more than anyone (he had a very "all-American" look and would not have been stuck in the crowd).

Clint and Meredith were interrogated by police and asked to undergo a polygraph examination, but Clint refused. Clint also hired a lawyer shortly after the investigation began. He has been fairly criticized for these reasons. Why do many people think he doesn't take a test if he has nothing to hide? Polygraphs, on the other hand, are notoriously unreliable. Having a lawyer only made Clint smarter. However, in these situations, people are always looking for someone to blame. There is no evidence that Clint wanted to hurt Bryan.

Two girls, who were seen talking to Brian, were also questioned by the investigator, but never asked to take a polygraph.

Brian's cell phone, credit card and bank account have not been used since the night he disappeared.

theory
There are too many theories around Brian's disappearance that I can't cover here. These are the combinations of the most popular theories I have found with my thoughts:

1. Bryan unknowingly escaped at the end of the night, encountering a foul play on his way home. The area was known to be particularly unsafe.

Description: Bryan was talking to the band while packing. The bar was closed and staff could have locked the front door after thinking that everyone had left without realizing that Brian was still there. After that, he was able to leave with members of the band and other staff, and began to go home alone when he encountered a fraudulent play.

Brian's case is often tied to smiley face killer theory. Smiley Face Killer theory became known when it was advocated by two retired NY detectives in 1997. The basic outline of the theory is that the body of a white college student (the exact number depends on the source, but I found roughly 45-50) drowned in water after a night out with a drinker. I found it. Males have been found in 11 states, primarily in the Midwest, especially Minnesota and Wisconsin. It is believed that these men were not accidentally drowned, but were forcibly drowned by successive murderers. , Wood or ground.

Personally, this theory occurs in so many places that it's unbelievable given that smiley faces are probably the most commonly drawn graffiti (which is pretty much everywhere). think. But there has been a fair amount of research on theory, and some take it seriously. If that is true, I don't think there is any one person who can kill these men. Surely it must be a killer or a group of people. Given that Brian's body has not been discovered, I don't think it really makes sense to classify Brian into this category.

2. Brian exits the emergency exit and goes to the construction site where he falls into a hole and faints. Then the hole was covered with cement.

Being so drunk, Brian could have thought it would be faster to get home through the construction site. However, if Brian accidentally fell into the hole, he was near the surface of the water, so the construction worker would have met him before pouring the cement.

3. Brian accidentally died in the bar. The staff at the bar were worried about the lawsuit and dragged him out of the emergency exit and disposed of his body.

This theory is supported by the fact that Brian has never been seen on a camera leaving an ugly tuna. Assuming staff left through the staff's exit, and no camera at this exit, this could work.

However, I also feel that many humans have been unable to handle such secrets. How many staff closed in the middle of the night? All of these people need to know that they are secretly hiding the corpse from the bar. Indeed, if this were to happen, one of those people would have cracked and told the authorities something about what happened that night. It is enough for one person to say something.

4. Brian disappears to start a new life.

Investigators have never actually found anything that suggests cheating. However, there was no activity on Brian's cell phone or bank account, and no cash was withdrawn after that night. Surely if he wanted to start a new life, he would have started with at least one of these. Also, given his call to Alexis and the plans to propose to her, he was clearly invested in their relationship. He would have had to make a rather sudden change of heart to leave completely.

Conclusion

I'm leaning towards the idea that Brian was somehow left unnoticed by the camera, then encountered a mischief and his body was destroyed. I don't think he died in an accident because I think his body was found. The surrounding areas and rivers that were thoroughly explored. I am very confused about this incident. The more I think about it, the more I get confused.

Aftermath

Alexis kept calling Brian for a few months, but it always went directly to voicemail, except once in September when the phone rang three times. She thought this could mean Brian's phone was turned on. But Brian's mobile phone provider rejected the theory as a glitch. Even after Brian's dad went missing, I think he continued to pay for his phone bill in case he was still there and decided to contact him.

Brian's father, Randy, died in a strange accident in September 2008. His obituary was published online and the public could comment on it. The comment surveyed was "I love you, Dad. Bryan (US Virgin Islands)." However, the comment turned out to be fake and was written from a public computer in Franklin County (where Columbus is).

In April 2018, the Ugly Tuna Salona closed after 14 years of operation.

Investigators continue to be plagued by this case. There is no example that left me with so many questions. It's very frustrating because it feels like you need to have such an obvious answer. How can someone be right there and leave like this:

What happened to Brian Scheffer?

4 THE DATING GAME KILLER

Bachelor's degree 1, contestant in "date game", film student, fashion photographer... sexual predator, rape criminal, serial murderer, death row prisoner.

A short note before you start: The timeline for this case is everywhere. To really understand the full picture of Alcala's horrific crime, I recommend reading it from start to finish. As always, read it carefully.

1943-1968
San Antonio, Mexico, Los Angeles
Alcala was born in 1943 in San Antonio, Texas. His family moved to Mexico at the age of eight. When Alcala was 11, his father decided to leave his family and support his mother and four children. After his father left, his mother moved his family to Los Angeles.

In 1960, when Rodney was 17, he joined the US military. He was diagnosed with a severe antisocial personality disorder and worked for four years before being discharged on medical grounds.

Upon leaving the Army in 1964, Alcala graduated with a degree in fine arts from UCLA and a bachelor's degree in 1968.

In the same year, eight-year-old Tali Shapiro was abducted on the way to school. I was lucky enough to see another driver seducing Tali into a car without a license plate and immediately felt bad about it. The driver chased the car to the apartment building and called the police. Police arrived and interrupted the apartment, discovering that Tari lay in a blood puddle and was raped and beaten within an inch of her life. Attempts were also made to strangle her with a metal rod.

Upon searching the apartment, police found it to belong to UCLA student Rodney Alcala. What I found in my apartment were photographic equipment and many pictures of the girl. But Alcala was not found anywhere.

runtime
1968-1971, New York City, New Hampshire
Alcala fled California as soon as possible. He acquired a new identity as'John Berger' and went to New York where he enrolled in NYU Film School. His associates saw him as free, lively and fun to love. While in NYU, he met Roman Polanski who trained him in photography. Alcala is an important skill that will later be used to seduce and trap victims.

Alcala also got a job as a camp counselor in an art camp for girls in New Hampshire. Here he changed his pseudonym to a slightly different name, John Burger. At the time, he was on the FBI Top 10 Most Wanted Fugitive list of rapes and attempted to kill Tali Shapiro, but his identity change allowed him to live unnoticed by law enforcement.

Inside and outside the prison
1971 – 1977, Los Angeles
In 1971, Alcala's luck changed. Two arts camp campers have confirmed counselors on a post office wanted poster. It was Rodney Alcala, not John Burger. They spoke to the camp director who informed the police. Alcala was immediately arrested and handed over to California. Tari Shapiro and her family moved to Mexico after she was attacked. That is, she had not been tried to testify Alcala. This had a huge impact on the prosecution's lawsuit. Tali's absence meant that he could not be convicted of rape and attempted a murder, and had to agree to offer Alcala a plea bargain instead. Alcala was found guilty of child abuse and sentenced to one year.

At that time, the US justice system was largely focused on the rehabilitation of criminals, leading to uncertain judgments. The Parole Commission has decided whether the inmates were adequately rehabilitated, and therefore whether they should be released. Alcala was able to convince the board that was attractive, smart and ready to re-enter society. He was released on parole after being placed in prison for just 34 months in 1974.

Two months after parole, Alcala told her 13-year-old girl to drive to school, so he got into the car. Instead, he drove a car with her and offered her a marijuana. She told police that she was abducted and fled. Alcala was not charged with kidnapping, but spent another two years in prison for parole and providing marijuana to minors.

Free again
1977, Los Angeles, New York City
After being released from prison, Alcala had no problems returning himself to society. He created his identity as a charming and charismatic fashion photographer and worked as a typesetter at the Los Angeles Times (which happened to be a convicted sex offender, but he had to wrap it up). Was very successful). He also persuaded the parole officer in Los Angeles and allowed him to travel to New York and "visit his family" (a very bad move).

Dating games
In September 1978, Alcala took part in the "Encounter Game" as a bachelor's degree 1. Alcala was his factor in the public eye and felt quite selfish about his deceptions against law enforcement and the public.

Host Jim Lange introduced Alcala as follows:

"The successful photographer who got his start when his father found him in a 13-year-old darkroom was fully developed."

If they knew they were aggressively killing women when Alcala wasn't attending the game show, this wouldn't have been so funny.

Alcala found it fascinating and entertaining, and "Bachelorette" Cheryl Bradshaw chose him for her date. However, the date finally didn't happen because Cheryl felt Alcala "creepy." Alcala was not content with the rejection, to say the least.

Robin Samsaw
June 20, 1979, Huntington Beach
In the summer of Southern California, 12-year-old Robin Samsoe had a great time. She had plenty of time on the beach and was looking forward to starting a ballet class. Robin was described as fun, sweet, affectionate and happy. She was very close to her mother Marianne. Robin loves to dance and has signed a contract with the town's ballet studio to answer the phone for

two hours in exchange for lessons.

Before heading to the studio that day, she arranged to meet her best friend Bridget on the beach. When they arrived, a dark-haired man with a camera approached them and asked them to take a picture of them. Robin said it was okay, but when the neighbor showed up and asked the girl if everything was okay, the man looked as if he had seen a ghost. He grabbed his camera and was gone before they knew it.

The girl left the beach and Robin noticed that she was likely to be late for the studio. Brigitte urged her to take her bike. Brigitte would be the last person to see Robin alive.

Later that day, a ballet studio employee called in to Robin's house and notified Marianne that Robin had never arrived at the studio. She called 911 immediately.

Twelve days later, Robin's body was discovered in the foothills of the San Gabriel Mountains. The San Gabriel Mountains are 40 miles north of where she last lived. The animal wrecked her body, leaving only bones.

The investigator interviewed Brigitte, and from her description, a sketch of a man from the beach was created and distributed throughout Southern California. The sketch was a good depiction of Alcala. As his parole officer in LA saw it, he notified Huntington Beach PD that they had to take a look at Rodney Alcala. Four days later, they looked for Alcala who lived in their mother's house. It was right next to where the Robin Ruins were found. They arrested him for murder.

Evidence for Alcala
Probably the most important evidence found at home was the receipt of a storage unit that Alcala had rented in Seattle nine days after Robin disappeared.

The investigator traveled to Seattle in search of a storage unit. They hit the gold and found hundreds of pictures of children and women. Neither Robin nor Bridget were included in either photo, but I found another girl photo taken at Sunset Beach, about two miles away from where Robin was abducted. This picture was taken even on the day Robin disappeared. The other teenage girls came out earlier and told police that they also approached them that day, at the beach, a long dark-haired man asked them to take a picture of them. They also found a small pouch filled with earrings. One pair confirmed by Robin's mother was that of her daughter.

Roller coaster continues, 1980-2003
The evidence for Alcala was overwhelming. In 1980, he was tried and sentenced to death for the killing of Robin Samsoe. But in 1984, the California Supreme Court overturned that belief. Alcala's second trial took place in 1986 and again he was sentenced to death.

In 1994, Alcala wrote a book titled "Jury" in which he declared innocence in the killing of Robin Samsoe.

In 2001, his belief was overturned...again.

In 2003, Alcala was shocked he didn't think he really would come. DNA analysis technology has taken a huge leap since the 1970s and has played an extremely important role in solving cold murder cases for decades.

Los Angeles, 1977-1979
Between November 1977 and June 1979, four women were brutally beaten, raped, strangled and left in a carefully placed state. These are:

The 18-year-old Jill Barcomb, who moved from New York to California three weeks ago, was discovered in the valley off the Mulholland Highway in November 1977.

27-year-old registered nurse Georgia Wiked found in an apartment in Malibu in December 1977.

Charlotte Lamb, a 32-year-old legal clerk, was found in a laundry room in an apartment building in El Segundo in June 1978.

Working as a computer program key punch operator, 21-year-old Jill Parento was found in a Burbank apartment in June 1979.

Alcala DNA was found in the murder scene of each woman. Charlotte Lamb DNA was also found in earrings found in a Seattle warehouse.

Third murder trial 2010

Alcala was tried a third time for the killing of Robin Samsoe. The prosecution demanded that Alcala's trial against the killing of Lokala be combined with the murder trial against Jill B, Georgia, Charlotte, and Jill P, which Alcala strongly protested. However, in 2006, the California Supreme Court granted a request to combine a murder trial.

In 2010, 66-year-old Alcala was tried in five murder cases. Alcala chose to represent herself, as Bundy did in a trial to murder a Florida student sister. The trial was a circus. Al-Kara asked in various voices for 5 hours. He claimed he was applying for a job as a photographer at Knott's Berry Farm on the day Robin disappeared, and claimed that the earrings identified as Robin's were him. Alcala was almost 100% focused on persuading a jury who was innocent about Robin's killing. Regardless of whether he killed four other women, he simply said "I didn't remember."

An eight-year-old girl, Tari Shapiro, who died after Alcala's rape in 1968, returned to protest against Alcala. Tari was never asked by Alcala. He simply apologized to her for his "despicable behavior".

In his final statement, Alcala made an interesting choice for the judges to play Arlo Guthrie's song "Alice's Restaurant". It goes:

Want to kill, want to kill

I want to see blood, blood, intestines, and veins in my teeth.

Eat dead charred body.

That is, kill, kill, kill, kill.

Not surprisingly, Alcala was convicted of all five murders and sentenced to death again.

In 1971, while Alcala was studying at a NYU film school, a 23-year-old transworld airline flight attendant, Cornelia Krilly, was found raped and strangled in an apartment in Manhattan. A bite was found on the left chest. In 1971, nothing really led an investigator into a Cornelia murderer. Alcala was not on their radar either. In New York, he was known as John Berger. But in

2010, these elements began to be properly placed. Knowing that Rodney Alcala was John Berger and was in New York City in 1971 gave the survey new hope. The fingerprint of the letter under Cornelia's body was entered into the FBI's database and matched with Alcala. The impression of Alcala's teeth also showed that the bite scar on Cornelia's chest was created by him. 39 years later, the Cornelia killing was resolved.

In 1978, the body of Ellen Jane Hover was found on the site of Rockefeller Estate in Westchester County. At the age of 23, he disappeared 11 months before July 1977 (remember when Alcala traveled to New York to visit his family?)

Ellen was a talented pianist, incredibly clever, and planning to go to medical school. Her father owned Ciro's, a famous Hollywood nightclub. Ellen was described by her family and friends as beautiful, sweet and authentic.

On July 15, 1977, Ellen wrote "John Burger" in her diary. She intended to see him for lunch that day, never to see him again. Many witnesses said they had seen Ellen talking to a man outside the apartment, consistent with Alcala's portrayal, for the days leading up to her disappearance, as well as the day she disappeared. Her friend asked her who was the "whimsical guy," and she replied, "Oh, he's okay. He's a photographer." He also Rockefeller Estate. It was seen when Ellen disappeared. At the time, Alcala was questioned by police about Ellen's disappearance and refused Polygraph. However, at that point, they had no bodies and the investigation was stalled.

In 2011, Alcala was sentenced to death for the killing of five Californians and was charged with the killing of Cornelia Krilly and Ellen Hover. In 2012 he was handed over to New York. To the surprise of the New York prosecutor, Alcala guilty of murdering both women. He was sentenced to two simultaneous sentences of 25 years in his life. After that, Alcala returned to California and was sentenced to death at the age of 75 today.

Unidentified photos
Remember the photos found in the storage lockers in Seattle, Alcala? In 2010, NYPD and Huntington Beach PD published 120 people to the public, hoping that people could step forward and identify the women and children in

them.

In 2013, Cathy Thornton came across Alcala's photo archive. Cathy's sister Christine went missing in the spring of 1977. Looking at the pictures, she found one of the women riding a motorcycle. After close examination, she was unquestionable for her being Christine. Kathy contacted Huntington Beach PD about her findings and submitted her DNA to the national missing database.

In 2015, her DNA was matched with a body found in Wyoming in 1982. The investigators discovered that Alcala had met Christine and agreed to ride with him and take a picture. The photo appears to have been taken not far from where her body was found. Alcala was charged with the killing of Christine Thornton in September 2016.

As of October 2016, 21 women have been identified in the photo collection. However, over 100 subjects in the photo remain unidentified.

These pictures are questioning, how many more lives did Rodney Alcala claim?

The photo archive is here.

Final thought

Alcala was a skilled manipulator and had an IQ close to that of a genius. This explains how he could (literally) escape the murder for so long. I just want to reiterate what I wrote in my last post about remembering victims of monsters like Rodney Alcala. After all, the world was taken away from them too soon into the hands of truly evil humans. I gave Robin, Jill, Georgia, Charlotte, Jill, Cornelia, Ellen, Christine (unfortunately there's more) more. I hope they are peaceful now.

Also, if the camera is approaching, you may be a model and you want to take you somewhere and take a picture of you. Please run in the opposite direction! Sure you are beautiful and you can be a model, but this guy is probably full of shit. Don't risk it.

5 THE MURDER OF SHANDA SHARER

Do you know of any terrible and incomprehensible cases that will accompany you? For me, this is the story of Shanda Sharer. This makes me angry at writing and also mad at reading. Therefore, be careful and continue. Especially, at the start and end of the disturbing part, * is added when skipping.

Shanda Renee Sharer was born on June 6, 1979 in Pineville, Kentucky. Her parents, Steven Shearer and Jacqueline Vought, divorced when Shanda was a child. Shanda was a close friend of her mother, and became close to her father and stepmother Sharon.

Shanda was the kind of girl you wanted to be friends with. She was cheerful, sociable and had a lot of fun. I used to play volleyball as a cheerleader at school. She was smart and had good results.

About Shanda's 12th birthday in June 1991, she and her mother moved to New Albany, Indiana.

Shanda began at Hazelwood Middle School in New Albany. At the beginning of the school year she fought 14-year-old Amanda Hebrin. The two were detained together where they solved the problem and became friends. Shanda's mother, Jackie, didn't settle for friendship. She's in trouble because Shanda's grades have gone off since it started.

Soon the friendship deepened and the two girls began exchanging love letters. In October, they took part in a school dance and met Amanda's ex-girlfriend, Melinda Loveless, 16 years old.

The scenes of Shanda and Amanda together frightened Melinda. In the dance, Melinda tried to fight Shanda, but Amanda stopped her. A few weeks later, Melinda publicly threatened Shanda and began writing to Amanda that she wanted Shanda's body.

Upon discovering Amanda's letter to Shanda, many of them were sexually explicit, and Jackie and Stephen decided to transfer Shanda to another school. By the end of November, Shanda enrolled in Our Lady's Eternal Help Catholic School.

When Shanda transferred to school, Shanda and Amanda were not split. Amanda continued to write to Shanda and called her home. But Shanda was distracted by her new school and wasn't as responsive as Amanda wanted.

jealousy

I was a teenage girl myself, but not so long ago, I feel tense more intensely, including jealousy, anger, and sadness. You might say you hate someone. Maybe even say that they want to be dead. You never really mean that.

For most high school students, school life is their entire world. The people they met played a central role in our lives at the time. For many, high school is a place where you experience your first relationship and make friends who you think will be forever close. However, when I look back on my high school days, the experiences that seemed like the end of the world at that time disappeared.

This is where this story makes a very dark turn. What looked like a jealous lover's spats in the last section was caught up in a much more sinister and malicious one. It causes the wicked acts that can change the lives of four people and end the lives of others.

Original average girl

Before getting into the event on January 10, 1992, let's take a quick look at the background of the people involved. Aphrodite Jones, author of Cruel Sacrifice, a true criminal book of 1994, which examines the Shanda Sharer case in detail, dubs four girls "The Original Mean Girls".

MELINDA LOVELESS, 16 years old

Melinda is from New Albany, Indiana. Her father, Larry Loveless, was a Veteran in Vietnam and had a hard time holding her job. The money he earned was directed to his motorcycle and gun. He was violent, verbally abusive, drunk and perverted.

Larry and Melinda's mother, Marjorie, had an "open relationship." Alternatively, Larry had his friends "rent" Marjorie for sex. The two were regularly engaged in orgy between men and women picked up at the bar. Larry raped Marjorie hard while his three daughters were at home and could hear everything. He once beaten Marjorie badly and was hospitalized. Marjorie repeatedly tried to commit suicide due to abuse.

Larry is also likely to have exposed his daughter to sexual abuse, although the extent of this is unknown. There are reports that he molested his daughter and niece when they were children. Melinda shared a bed with him until she was 14 years old.

Marjorie and Larry divorced when Melinda was 14 years old. Larry moved to Florida, where he had little contact with his family.

Melinda suffered from depression and had to fight regularly, both of which were largely caused by her difficult family life. This affected her schooling and she had to repeat her school for a year. Melinda was open about her lesbian orientation, which was rare in the little town of Indiana in the early 1990s.

LAURIE TACKETT (17 years old)
Raleigh is from Madison, Indiana and was about 50 miles from New Albany. She comes from a strict fundamentalist Christian family. Her father worked in a factory. Raleigh's parents were abusive and both orphanages visited the house several times.

Raleigh was fascinated by paranormal phenomena and vampires. Early in 1991, at the age of 16, Laurie began self-harm and she was hospitalized several times. She was admitted to a mental ward and was diagnosed with borderline personality disorder. In September 1991, Raleigh dropped out of high school.

While living in Louisville in October, Laurie met Melinda and became a friend. By the end of the year, Raleigh spent most of his time with New Albany and Melinda in Louisville, and seldom returned to Madison.

HOPE RIPPEY (15 years old)

Hope was from Madison and was friends with Raleigh, but her parents didn't like Hope to spend with Raleigh. Hope and Tony have been intimate since very young. Hope also results in self-harm.

TONI LAWRENCE, 15 years old
Toni was born and raised in Madison. She was on good terms with Hope but didn't know the other girls. There are reports that Tony was raped when he was 14, but I couldn't find much information on this. Like Raleigh and Hope, Toni also self-harmed.

June 10-11, 1992
On the night of the 10th, Raleigh, Hope and Tony were supposed to get into Raleigh's car and go to a rock concert. This is the first time Toni has met Raleigh. Raleigh didn't look or act like a regular 90s teenage girl. She had a harsh white blonde boyish haircut and was wearing black from head to toe. She had an ominous and inaccessible look and showed little emotion. Tony soon got an uneasy atmosphere from Raleigh.

Laurie asked Hope, "Have you told her yet?" "What do you want to tell her?"

"We are going to kill the girl tonight."

Toni didn't know what to think. She thought it was a kind of twisted joke.

Before heading to the concert, Raleigh drove to New Albany to pick up Melinda. Hope didn't know Melinda well, and Toni had never seen her. Melinda was beautiful, glamorous and excited to meet the girls. She got in a car with a big knife and told Hope and Toni that she wanted to be like her and stole her girlfriend, so she "wanna scare" this girl Shanda. Laurie, Hope, and Tony have never met Shanda before.

The four arrived at Shanda's house around 8 pm and Melinda hid on the floor of the car. When Shanda looked at her, she knew she was scared and wouldn't come with her. Laurie and Melinda told Hope and Toni to knock on Shanda's door and ask her to go see Amanda.

Shanda has never seen these girls, but wanted to see Amanda. She told them to go home at midnight when their parents fell asleep.

Hope and Toni returned to their car and went to a rock concert. Around 12:00 they drove back to Shanda's house. Along the way, Melinda described how excited she was to kill Shanda, but also said she just wanted to scare her. Hope and Toni did not believe that Melinda had plans to kill the girl, but Toni became more and more worried. She refused to go to the door with Hope and brought them to Shanda.

Hope returned with Shanda, and they got into the car and started talking about Amanda. Hope explained that Amanda was waiting for them at the Witches Castle in Utica, Indiana. Melinda then jumped behind Shanda, grabbed her hair and attached the knife's blunt tip to her throat. Shanda screamed and begged Melinda not to hurt her. Melinda yelled, "Shut up, bitch!" and began asking Shanda about her sexual relationship with Amanda.

At the Witch's Castle, Melinda and Laurie bound Shanda. Laurie scared Shanda by telling her how the place was full of dead people. Shanda was scared and asked him to go home. Raleigh lit up her T-shirt with a bright smile and disdained Shanda for provocation.

They left Shanda and the Witch's Castle to find an open gas station. Shanda talked about a person near her house. They went there, but she covered her with a blanket because Laurie knew that Shanda might flee or seek help if she was near her house. Later, they drove further into the woods not far from Raleigh's house.

*Torture has begun here. Laurie and Melinda punched Shanda, kicked her, and tried to cut her throat with a knife, but they weren't sharp enough. They used it to stab her chest and abdomen. Hope and Toni stayed in the car, but Hope temporarily got out of the car to help hold Shanda in restraint. Melinda and Laurie strangled Shanda with a rope and killed her until she fainted. They put her in the trunk and drove back to Raleigh's house. They told Hope and Toni that Shanda was dead.

When Laurie found Shanda noisy, he returned to the car and stabbed her until it was quiet. Melinda and Raleigh then drove the countryside, leaving Hope and Tony in Raleigh's house.

Each time Shanda made a noise, Raleigh went around the trunk, stabbed her with a knife, and beat her with a tire iron. The length of time they were driving is unknown.

They returned to Raleigh's house, picked up Hope and Toni, then returned to the forest. Laurie and Melinda wanted to show what Hope and Toni did to Shanda, but Toni refused to see. Seen by three girls, Hope sprayed Shanda with Windex. She said, "You don't look so hot right now, right?"

At the gas station, Tony bought a large bottle of Pepsi and drank it, but Raleigh picked it up and emptied it.

They drove north to the country road, Lemon Road, surrounded by fields. Laurie and Hope wrapped the still alive Shanda in a blanket and carried her to the edge of the field, still visible from the road. Laurie gasped Shanda from a Pepsi bottle and lit her. *

The four girls left McDonald's for food. Toni is hysterical, using a payphone to call a friend and talk about the murder. Melinda and Raleigh decide that Tony needs to go home.

Melinda dropped off Toni and Hope at home, then contacted Amanda and told her that Shanda was dead. Amanda did not believe it and agreed to meet later. Laurie and Melinda picked up Amanda and then returned to Melinda's house. At home, Melinda cried hysterically and told Amanda what she had done to Shanda. Amanda didn't believe it yet, but when she showed the trunk of Raleigh's car, the situation changed. There was a lot of blood inside, such as bloody handprints, hair, and Shanda's socks. Amanda was in fear and was required to take her home.

Investigation
When the girl was in McDonald's, the brothers of Don and Ralph were out looking for a quail. They passed the Jefferson Proving Ground and ran on a country road for about eight miles. There they found a large dark object by the side of the road. As they approached, Don thought it was a bomb doll. They looked closer and found that it was the burned body of a young woman. It reminded Dong of his time in Vietnam. They returned home, called police, and asked them to return to the site of the body until the sheriff arrived.

Around 12 pm Deputy Sheriff Randle Spry arrived, followed shortly by

Jefferson County Sheriff Buck Shippley. Detective Steve Henry and Sergeant Curtis Wells, a forensic expert, arrived around 1pm.

* 4 men couldn't believe in the horrifying sights. The girl's body was burned unknowingly and "raised" in a sexual way, and Wells was convinced she was probably sodomized. *

Meanwhile, Shanda's father, Steve, awoke. He noticed Shanda wasn't in her room, but didn't think much. He thought she was sleeping in a family room in the basement. He began to worry when he realized that she wasn't there. He first called Shanda's friend and then his ex-wife, Jackie, told her she couldn't find Shanda. Jackie came in and submitted a report of the missing person. After that, Jackie, Steve, and Steve's wife, Sharon, searched the area for Shanda.

About 8:20 pm, the hysterical Tony entered the police station with his father. She hurried and told Detective Henry to tell him everything as soon as possible. She told Henry about plans to go to a rock concert with Raleigh and Hope, and they eventually went to New Albany to pick up Raleigh's friend Melinda. She knew the girl's name was Shanda and she was 12 or 13 years old. I couldn't remember the exact timing, but Witch's Castle, Woods, Raleigh's House, Raleigh and Melinda defeated Shanda in the trunk, filling the petrol station with petrol.

Toni remembered Shanda's address. Henry contacted Wells to see if the missing person's report had been filed at that address. There was one 12-year-old Shanda Sharer. The description of Shanda in the missing person's report was consistent with the body found earlier in the day. The dental record was then used to clearly identify the body as belonging to Shanda.

Raleigh and Melinda were arrested on January 12, 1992.

Judgment
All four girls were charged as adults. They each accepted plea bargaining to avoid the death penalty.

Laurie and Melinda were both sentenced to 60 years in Indiana Women's Prison.

In a 2004 appeal, Hope's decision was shortened from 60 years to 35 years.

Toni was found guilty of one of the criminal confinements and was sentenced to up to 20 years.

Aftershock

Steve Shearer, who was completely overwhelmed by the murder of his daughter, could not continue. He found his only escape from drinking in 2005 and died of alcohol abuse. He was 53 years old.

During Melinda's trial hearing, the dreadful abuse of her father Larry Loveless revealed her family. In February 1993, he was charged and arrested for rape, sodomy, and sexual violence. He spent two years in prison awaiting trial. However, because of the state of restriction (5 years in Indiana), most of these particular crimes occurred up to 25 years ago, so the judge said that Larry was guilty of one sexually violated crime. Withdrew all charges. He was convicted and released in June 1995. I'm sorry, but I wasn't honest.

While in prison, Melinda has been involved in training service dogs. She is well known for training in the ICAN (Indiana Canine Assistance Dogs) program and is often asked to help dogs that are difficult to train. Charlie Petrizzo, a victim of burns raising an ICAN service dog, contacted Shanda's mother about Melinda. Together they watched a video of Melinda training her dog in prison. Watching the video, Jackie said:

"She (Melinda) was sincere. She was considerate. In the ICAN program she has something that she can show love in her life and there is no betrayal on either side."

In 2012, Jackie made an unexpected decision to donate the puppy Angel to Melinda to train for ICAN in honor of Shanda.

release

Toni was released on parole in 2000 after working for eight years.

Hope was paroleed in 2006, where he served for 14 years.

On the 26th anniversary of Shanda's death, January 11, 2018, Raleigh was released on parole.

Melinda will be released in September 2019.

Murder drive
I researched the case in depth, watched interviews, documentaries, read Aphrodite Jones's cruel sacrifice and reports online, and made a lot of reflections about it myself. I'm not saying that these ideas are original and never thought of. It is certainly so. But what, in my own words, was the main cause of this horrific crime? Also, I'm not saying here that any of these things I discuss do or justify what happened to Shanda.

Pack mentality
In this case, Melinda was an Alpha woman. But did Melinda abduct, torture and kill Shanda himself? Most definitely. She needed to back up from others to streamline her actions to herself. As far as I know, enter Raleigh who doesn't make any resistance or tells Melinda not to kill Shanda. She even encouraged Melinda, saying she would help. Raleigh was the most violent of the four girls. Both Melinda and Raleigh had what the other needed. Melinda was jealous of her wanting Shanda to die, but she couldn't kill herself. Laurie didn't even know Shanda. She just had a bloody desire and wanted to know what it was like to kill someone. Is the match made in hell different?

Even without Hope and Toni, it is quite possible that Melinda and Laurie could move forward by killing Shanda. Shanda never gets hurt by himself, but he is involved in bullying Shanda and tried to "help" by detaining Raleigh and Melinda. She also invited Shanda into the car. Hope Hope wanted to impress Raleigh, but perhaps even worse than her.

Toni was the toughest murder case. Her crime was that she had never tried to stop others. But Tony never met Raleigh or Melinda, and both girls were older and intimidating. She saw Laurie and Melinda torturing Shanda, and perhaps "what could happen to me if I stopped doing this?"

Domination and domination
Melinda really couldn't control her life. Her father was abusive and the family lived in fear of him. She was fooling around school and had to go back a year ago. Then her ex-girlfriends, who she was still emotional, met with a much younger girl. Having the power to control Shanda can be said to

have felt Melinda in control when everything else in her life fell apart, even for a short time.

But, on the other hand, the torture and hell they afflicted Shanda suggest a loss of total control and consideration of human life.

Natural VS training

I'm not a psychologist and I'm not studying phenomena other than murder studies, so I don't want to dive deep into the discussion of nature and parenting. But Melinda did a particularly bad job. She probably experienced verbal and emotional abuse from her father on a daily basis, and I'm sure the abuse went even further than that. Her father was sexually and physically violent against her mother and did nothing to hide it.

The questions we have to ask ourselves are: Would the situation have changed if the girls had a more stable family life, or were Laurie and Melinda predisposed to violence?

I also know enough to say that the vast majority of people who grow sexually, physically and emotionally persistently are not murderers. I know that it is possible to completely change the experiences of abuse and turn them into positive ones. For example, an abused person often helps someone who is experiencing a similar situation because he can better understand where he came from.

But I have to cover all the locations, right?

In this case, I think I covered everything I planned. I knew it was hard to write about (it's never easy in a real crime!) To be honest, it made me emotionally and seriously tired. I'm a little wondering how to get this done. I honestly tell Shanda's story, and when people read this, we hope they see Shanda for the shining star she was (and still is). I also overcame a lot with the admiration of Shanda's mother, Jackie. Shanda's mother lost her daughter in the worst way we could imagine, but she was able to stay strong and see the light no matter what. She will donate the puppies to Melinda for training in prison, she said:

"It's my choice. She's my kid. If you don't bring good from bad, nothing will get better. And I know what my kid wants My child wants this."

6 THE MURDER OF
JOANNA YEATES

Happiness, cleanliness, and success-three words to describe her even if you don't know Joanna Yeates. After Joanna's disappearance on December 17, 2010, her face began to appear on the cover of almost every tabloid in Britain, and the British civilian could quickly learn more about her 25-year-old life. I was able to find it. ..

Joanna was not the type you would simply expect to disappear. She was sensible and was a good landscaper, never taking too much or taking medicine. She has a family and had a stable relationship with her boyfriend Greg Leadon (27), who has been dating for two years. They have lived together for over a year and in October 2010 Greg, Joanna and their pet cat moved together to a new apartment on 44 Canynge Road in Clifton, just outside Bristol. Overall, life seemed good for Joanna.

The night when everything changed

December 17th was Friday, it was approaching Christmas and the atmosphere was festive. Greg was visiting the Sheffield family on the weekend. That night, Joanna joined a colleague for a drink after work. She left the Ram Pub at about 8pm and went home. A surveillance video on her way home, she went to the Waitrose supermarket and left without buying anything. At 8:30, she called her friend Rebecca to arrange a meeting on Christmas Eve. Joanna was watched on the surveillance video at about 8:40 on the Tesco Express and bought a pizza there. Then she went to an unlicensed bargain boo and bought two ciders.

Joanna is missing

Greg returns to his apartment and finds a cat that appears to be unfed. There was no sign of Joanna. He called her cell phone, which rang from within her coat pocket. Greg also discovered Joanna's purse, glasses, and keys. At around midnight on December 18, he became very concerned and reported that Joanna was missing to police and her parents.

In the flat, the researcher found a receipt for the pizza that Joanna purchased. Oddly, the pizza package wasn't retrieved, suggesting she didn't eat it, but the pizza itself wasn't found anywhere. Both cider bottles were recovered, one partially consumed and the other unopened. There were no signs of forcible entry or disturbances inside the flat.

Investigators also examined Greg's laptops and cell phones as part of the standard protocol. I couldn't find anything disgusting.

By December 21, clues about Joanna's whereabouts were unclear. Joanna's parents, David and Teresa, made an emotional plea at a press conference, believing in their sudden disappearance. They contacted Joanna and asked her to express her love for her and her concerns about her safety. Joanna's brothers Chris and Greg were also present.

The body was discovered
By the 23rd, Joanna's family and Greg were convinced that the worst had happened. Joanna has been missing for 6 days. Her father expressed concern that Joanna might have been kidnapped from her apartment after her return.

On Christmas Day, their worst nightmare was confirmed. That morning, a couple walking a dog along Longwood Lane in Failand (about 4 miles from Joanna's apartment in Clifton) found a body on the side of a snow-covered road.

On the 26th, the body found was confirmed to belong to Joanna. Post-mortem examination also began that day, but the results were delayed due to the frozen body of Joanna. By 28th, the pathologist determined that the cause of death was strangulation. There was no evidence that Joanna had been sexually assaulted. Joanna was fully dressed, but she was not wearing a coat and was missing one sock. The socks were long gray ski socks. It was not found near her flat or where her body was found. Socks became an important part of the investigation, and criminals believe that the murderer may have kept it as a trophy.

Murder investigation
Landlord

Christopher Jeffreys, an English teacher who retired at Clifton College, a 65-year-old local private school, was well known in the community. Jeffreys is the owner of Joanna and Greg and lived in the apartment above them. He was an active participant in the local Liberal Democratic Party, helping with the campaign and being deeply involved in Clifton's neighborhood watch program. Jeffreys had an eccentric personality and sometimes made bold statements such as dyeing his hair blue. A former student described him as an unconventional but exciting teacher.

Jeffreys was involved in the Joannay Eighties murder investigation when asked about the allegations he had made to his neighbors when he drove out of Joanna's apartment around 9 pm. did. Neighbors told investigators that Jeffreys had said he saw Joanna, but Jeffries revealed that he hadn't seen Joanna clearly, only three. did.

From my reading of this case, Jeffries couldn't bother about what Jeffries was just irritating, simply by looking at Joanna outside her apartment that night. However, Jeffries was arrested on murder charges early in the morning of December 30, 2010.

The media spent a day of war over the arrest of Jeffreys. There was no other reason than this, other than the fact that Jeffries was indeed strange and wacky. Guardian columnist Stephen Moss said:

Britain's tatters (ie "Sun", "Daily Mail", "Daily Mirror"), such as "Professor Strange", "The Strange Mr Jeffries", the murdered owner of Joanne Nayates, "Suspect Peeping Tom". On the front page of, there were slanderous headlines. "

Jeffreys was released on bail on January 1, 2011, after being criminally questioned for two days. Not surprisingly, Jeffries sued eight British newspapers for defamation after he was no longer suspected in a murder investigation. His lawyer talked about the matter:

"Christopher Jeffries is the latest victim of regular witch hunts and character assassinations done by the worst elements of British tabloid media."

Jeffreys received not only "substantial damage" from the documents, but also a public apology from the police.

Real killer

Vincent Tabak is a 32-year-old Dutchman who worked as an engineer in Bristol. He lived in the apartment next to Joanna and Greg with his girlfriend Tanja Mawson. Police knocked Mr Tabak at about 4 am on December 18, after Greg reported that Joanna was missing. Tabak was asked if he knew anything about Joanna's disappearance. He answered that he did not.

Police searched Tabac's apartment on the 23rd. He was supportive, and during the investigation he found nothing of interest to him. Tabac and Mawson visited Cambridge on the 24th to stay with their family. On the same day, Tabak talked to the detective on the phone and said he was up all night until he went out to pick up his girlfriend early in the morning on the 18th. He also told them that he didn't know Joanna.

On the 28th, Tabac and Mawson drove to the Netherlands via Eurotunnel to spend the New Year with their family. The two saw a news report during the Netherlands about the fact that Jeffries was arrested on the day of the alleged killing in the Netherlands.

Tabak saw the opportunity to assemble Jeffreys, which turned out to be his biggest mistake. He called the detective, giving him information that Jefferies had gone out many times on the night Joanna disappeared, and said he saw him turn the car in different directions. DC Current Thomas flew to Holland the next day and spoke to Tabac for six hours. Tabaku began to look suspicious during the encounter. He said he changed versions of what he did that night and went out to Asda, not only to pick up his girlfriend, but to take a picture of the snow. He also seemed overly curious about the forensic tests being performed. At the request of DC Thomas, Tabak provided DNA samples and collected fingerprints.

Returning to England on January 2, 2011, Tabak was convinced he would be arrested. Only early on January 20, Tabac knocked on the door and was arrested for the killing of Joanne Nieates. Forensic examination revealed the presence of Tabac DNA in the body. Tabak alleged that the DNA results were forged by corrupt officials trying to frame him, but he quickly let go.

On January 22, Tabak was charged with the murder of Joanne Naiez, a few days after criminal interrogation. On February 8, he admitted to a prison minister that he had killed her.

On May 5, Tabac condemned the manslaughter but denied the murder. His manslaughter was dismissed and decided to be charged with murder in October 2011.

trial
The trial began 10 October 2011 in front of a jury and Justice Field.

During the investigation and trial, Tabak claimed that he was unaware that Joanna had all injuries to his neck, torso, head and arms (43 total).

The prosecution spoke of Tabak's intention to kill Joanna when she invaded her apartment that night. It wasn't an accident. Tabak was alleged to have applied "enough force" to strangle her. In other words, he may have stopped, but not.

Tabak's defense was that the killing was not sexually motivated and was not intended to kill him. He said she made a "flirty comment" to him and invited him for a drink in her apartment. When we got inside, he tried to kiss her, and she cried. He put his hand on her mouth to stop her screaming. He released his hand, but she continued to scream, so he put his hand around her throat with her mouth and the other hand and held it there, causing her to die unintentionally. It was

Then he tied her body in the trunk of the car and drove to Asda, who bought beer and potato chips. He sent a text to his girlfriend saying he was "bored". He then drove to Longwood Lane and abandoned the bodies found on Christmas Day.

The jury deliberated for three days and convicted 10-2 majority Tabak in the killing of Joanna Yates.

Tabak was sentenced to 20 years in prison. During his ruling, Justice Field talked about "sexual elements" that were part of the killing.

During the trial, the jury had never seen violent pornography on Vincent Tabak's computer, which he saw on his computer until the murder. Details of this were revealed after the trial. After the trial, it was discovered that Tabak also possessed pornographic images of more than 100 children. He was sentenced to another ten months in prison.

Aftermath

A memorial garden was planted where Joanna had previously worked to celebrate her memory.

Joanna was designing the new Southmead Hospital yard when she was killed. A plan was made to mourn Joanna in the garden.

After Tabac was convicted of the killing of Joanna, her father David said the murderer had been charged but this did not result in the closure of his family.

"I didn't realize that Joe had such an impact on others, and that it gave me so much pride. She died at the age of 25."-David Yates.

7 THE SOHAM MURDERS

I wanted to write about this case for a while. What I write is generally very sad and tragic, but it's a bit more personal to me as this is the first murder I really recognized properly. Before that, I didn't really think about whether the world was a safe place, but when I was eight, I saw the media reports of the incident and decided it wasn't safe. There are good people in the world, but definitely bad people.

The case I'm referring to is the killing of 10-year-old Holly Wells and Jessica Chapman (also known as Soham Murders) in 2002. The case is known for two photos taken on the day of the murder, two girls armed with each other in Manchester United red football shirts. Holly is a blonde and Jessica is a brunette. Both of them look happy.

Murder
August 4, 2002. The girls had barbecues with their family and friends, but like the children, they bored and left at around 6:15 pm. Soham, Cambridgeshire is a small town with about 11,000 people. I live in a small town with nearly 17,000 people. Regularly look at the same face and make a small chat with a smile. Soham is small, so I think seeing and greeting every day is almost the same. You trust your neighbor. After about 15 minutes, the girls disappeared. At 8:30, when the girl's parents went to check them, they couldn't find them anywhere. They were reported missing at 9:45 pm.

On subsequent days, the incident became national news. I appealed to the public to appeal before any information about the missing girl. The search team scrutinized the area for the signs. Soham locals were interviewed by the media and described their shock about what was happening. One such person interviewed at Sky News and the BBC was 29-year-old Ian Huntley.

Huntley was a caretaker at Soham Village College, a local secondary school, who lived in a villa in the schoolyard during the murder. He lived with his girlfriend Maxine Kerr. Huntley managed to work at school despite his previous allegations of rape and sex with underage girls.

Maxine left the town on August 4, and Huntley was at home alone. When he saw the two girls walking by the house, he invited them in and told them that their teacher, Max Kinkur, was inside. The girls are believed to have stayed at home for less than 20 minutes when Huntley killed them.

On her way back, Maxine also spoke to the media. In a statement, she accused her of "just going home," and when she mentioned Holly Wells in her past tense, she told police that she was just a really nice girl. I doubted.

Investigation
Police received some hints about the whereabouts of the girls in the days following their disappearance, but these showed little promise.

On August 16, 12 days after the girls were missing, police interrogated Huntley and Kerr separately. The question lasted seven hours, after which Huntley and Kerr stayed at the police station while searching for their home and the surrounding schoolyards. What they found is that Huntley is strongly involved in the disappearance of girls. Among the evidence found was a Manchester United shirt worn on the day of the missing, probably cut from the girl's body, as evidenced by the jagged edges of the material. They were burnt, found, and thrown into the trash in the schoolyard. This is the first time that police have expressed concern that girls may have been killed.

The next day, on the 17th, two bodies were found in Lake Heath, Suffolk. They have been removed from the site for further forensic testing as they were too degraded to be identified on site. On August 21, they were officially identified as Holly and Jessica.

Huntley is charged
Huntley was arrested on August 20, 2002 and charged with two murder charges. Huntley said in court during the trial that the dead were accidental. He claimed to have asked the girl to his house when he saw Holly bleeding. When Holly accidentally fell into the bath and drowned, he was helping Holly clear her bloody nose. When Jessica discovered what was happening, she screamed and began to call for help using the phone. But before she

contacted anyone, Huntley panicked and choked her to stop her screams.

Huntley then moved the body to the ditch and later discovered it. He later returned to his body and admitted that he had set them on fire in an attempt to destroy the forensic evidence. However, there was evidence of when the bodies were ditched, as shown by analysis of soil chemistry by forensic ecologist Patricia Wiltshire.

The jury dismissed the allegations that Huntley's death was accidental. Of the 12 juries, 11 believed he had killed the girl. On December 17, 2003, Huntley was sentenced to two life imprisonments. He has spent at least 40 years in prison and is not eligible for parole until 2042.

Maxine Kerr was sentenced to three and a half years in prison, claiming he had been with him on the night of the killing, overwhelming the path of justice by offering Huntley a fake alibi. Kerr was released after serving half the sentence. At the time of her release, Kerr was given a whole new identity. She is one of the former British prisoners who was admitted this.

today

Sixteen years have passed since Holly and Jessica were killed. I'm 23 now, but I'm really thinking about them because of my interest in true crime. I don't even live near where it happened, but in my morning morning newspaper I prepared for a school whose face is permanently branded in my head. I'm used to seeing their pictures. They were very similar in age to me and I looked like a girl who could easily be friends. It still hurt my mind when I thought about it. I'm happy to finally write about them and bring something into their memory. Sweet angels, I wish you were at peace.

8 CHRISTY MIRACK

Christy, 25, beautiful inside and out, was always described by her friends as positive and optimistic about life. She was deeply concerned with her family, friends and students teaching at Rollerstown Elementary School in Lancaster County, Pennsylvania. In return, she was loved and loved by everyone she met.

Christie lived in a three-bedroom townhouse with a female roommate in East Lampeter Township. The population at that time was about 16,000, and it is almost the same today. Known as the Amish country of Pennsylvania, the region is surrounded by rural areas and fields.

Christie spent the night preparing for her next school day. She prepared Christmas gifts for grade 6 and wrote notes for each. Since she was a kid she wanted to be a teacher and practiced by giving play lessons to her two brothers. At the age of 25, Christie lived the life she dreamed of as a girl. Tragically, this life was deprived of her in the most brutal and mean way unimaginable.

Murder
December 21, 1992. Christie wakes up Monday and is ready for the next week. Her roommate was already on the job when Christie was preparing to leave for her usual 7:45 am. She prepared for the cold winter breeze and collected presents for her students. When she was grabbed and pushed back into the apartment, she barely went outside.

At 9am, school days were about to begin, and Christie's students were waiting for her in the classroom. Worried when Christie didn't arrive, principal Harry Goodman called her home. The phone rang. When I called again after a while, the same thing happened.

Christie's house was near the school, so Principal Goodman decided to go and inspect her. When Goodman arrived home, the door was a little halfway open. When he pushed it open, he faced a horrifying sight of Christie lying on the floor. She was beaten, strangled and naked from the waist. Gifts to her students were scattered on her dead body.

Crime scenes said little about Christie's murderer. There were no signs of forced invasion, and Christie was beaten by an object removed from inside the house. Semen-shaped DNA from Christy's attackers was found on the carpet under Christy and on the body itself. It was then collected and made into evidence. All that the attacker left behind, but the investigators of the time had little hope.

Investigation
In the years following Christie's murder, the search for murderers made little progress. A description of the suspect and possible suspect cars has been published. No lead appeared. Police interviewed more than 1,500 suspects. By 1995, forensic testing performed on DNA found in the field had ruled out 60 people.

In 2007, Christie's younger brother, Vince, who decided to use Christie's memory to encourage people to continue talking about her, posted a sign on Route 30 in Lancaster County to discuss Christie's horrific day. I asked for information. He opened a Facebook page for his sister in 2009. There, people could share information about her memories and incidents.

New hope for the case
Investigators were struggling with where to proceed with the investigation of the Chirsty murder case, after years of tips and leads gone nowhere. In March 2017, they decided to contract Parabon NanoLabs, which specializes in DNA phenotyping, a technique used to predict an individual's appearance based on DNA sequence. Investigators sent to Parabon the semen sample found on the carpet at Christie's house. By November 2017, Parabon had produced an image outlining what Christie's killer would look like at the ages of 25, 45, and 55. Since these are only estimates, we did not consider environmental factors that could affect the appearance of the individual. Lancaster County investigators began turning images in the hope that someone might be able to recognize the individual.

May 2018. Parabon uploaded Christie's Killer DNA sequences to the database GEDmatch. It compares DNA sequences to find possible relatives or ancestors of an individual. Databases like GEDmatch are open to the public, anyone can voluntarily submit their DNA, and sequences are added to the database. It can then be used for a variety of purposes, such as creating a family tree, which can be useful in criminal investigations.

In late May, Parbon notified investigators in the Christy Mirack case that they found a very important match with the DNA sequence in the GEDmatch database. Individuals with a DNA match are likely to be relatives of Christy Mirack's murderer.

Progress after 26 years

Investigators examined this individual for whom DNA was on a database to see if any relatives lived in or near the area. They narrowed the search to a man, Raymond Row, 49. Raymond Row was 24 years old in 1992 because he lived just four miles from where he was when he was killed.

Rowe was, in fact, like a minor celebrity in the area. He was a DJ at small and large clubs in and around Lancaster County, hosting up to 800 dance parties on Friday and Row providing music. Rowe was named DJ Freez and was the owner of his company, Freez Entertainment. He also ran his own "DJ school" and DJ equipment rental store.

Undercover investigation

The evidence that Parabon provided for Lowe's involvement in the murder was not sufficient to convict him. I needed to take a step further. On May 31, Raymond Rowe was DJing at a local school dance. Detectives covered the line and watched Row act. When the event was over and Rowe was ready to leave, he threw out the water bottle and chewing gum, and investigators retrieved him when he was gone.

The bottle and gum were taken to the lab for a forensic test. We found DNA for an item that matched what was found in Christie's apartment. In fact, the odds that it wasn't him were 1 in 200 octillion. Twenty-six years later, Lancaster County police were able to arrest the Christie Milak murder case.

On Monday, June 25, 2018, Raymond Row was arrested in a murder case and was not released on bail. Yesterday, September 21, Rowe's trial date was set for the following May.

Christy justice

Christie's older brother Vince described it as a "bittersweet" day for him and his family. 26 years after not knowing who killed Christy, the family was finally able to close. There are still no indications why Rowe many years ago Christy again committed this brutal crime. At least now he will pay for his actions.

Christie's Facebook page, created by her brother Vince, is still active and is posted regularly. Many years later, people still write how much they miss Christie and love her. They talk about the memories they shared with her and post some fun time pics with them. Of course, I didn't know Christy, but reading about her felt me, maybe like another life. The important thing to think of is that Christie has much more than a horrible death. We must not forget that it brightened the days of the people around us with a bright smile and radiance.

This case was very interesting to study.

9 THE JAMISON FAMILY DEATHS

The case has been the subject of intense debate among Internet professionals for nine years, and throughout the true criminal community. To this day, the uncertainty surrounding it is very high. There are many questions that are likely to be unanswered. It's as wacky and weird as they come.

The case I'm referring to is the disappearance of three members of the Jamison family, Bobby (44), Sherilyn (40) and Madison (6), from Panoroa Mountain, Oklahoma, in October 2009. In 2013, the remaining three (terribly disassembled and skeletonized) were discovered sideways and face down in the soil.

Before it disappears
What I learned from reading about this case was that Jamison was not hesitant to do anything unconventional. Shortly before they disappeared, they began a survey of areas where they could escape Euphora's home in Oklahoma and purchase land to build a new life. What they found was a 40-acre parcel of OK Panorama Unten.

Jamison's family life was in turmoil leading to their disappearance. With chronic back pain from a 2003 car accident, Bobby had a negative impact on his mood. Sheriline was suffering from bipolar disorder, so she was given medication but not regularly. This caused her to get angry with the people around her and cause a seizure of severe depression. For these reasons, the marriage between Bobby and Sherilyn was tense. This was thought to be one of the main reasons they moved and re-planned.

Jamison was very private. Often, even the people closest to them didn't know what was really happening in their lives. Both Bobby and Sherilyn were very religious and were deeply involved in spirituality. But the two were paranoid that their home was invaded by spirits. They got to know a preacher who confessed about their concerns. Sheriline believed that the spirits were in and talking to Madison, as Madison was regularly talking to someone called Emily who wasn't there. But this was probably Madison's coping mechanism to deal with the disruption of family life. Bobby had his own concerns about spirits and asked the preachers if he knew where to buy "special bullets" to shoot some spirits on the roof of the house.

A storage container was placed on the characteristics of Yufaula. Jamison planned to bring with them when they started a new life. Perhaps the idea was that they lived there until they built a real house on the mountain. Due to the graffiti that sheriline sprayed, the storage unit caught the attention of Jamison's neighbor in Eufora-Sherrilin believed this to be a witch and told her neighbor. She also did a show with her friend Niki Shenord, who admitted that she did not take it so seriously on her own, but Sherilyn did not. In the storage unit, Sheryllin wrote her strange weird ramblings: "The black cat was poisoned" and "The witch didn't like it when the cat was killed." She was convinced that her neighbor had killed the cat, and didn't hesitate to let people know about it. Not surprisingly, this made the neighbor very uncomfortable and the family did their best without any sacrifice. Finally, this worked for Sherilyn because she really wanted to be alone.

A few weeks before the family's disappearance, considering Bobby's back pain, the couple decided to help a male boarder lift the heavy objects around the house. However, shortly after moving in, the border areas began to strain Sherilyn more and more. Sherilyn was disgusted by her border as she sat on the sofa next to her while Bobby was out and stood near her face because of Indian blood he was a white supremacist I told Niki that I was telling her Sherilyn was part of Native American. Very uncomfortable, Sherilyn fled to another room, where she picked up a gun. When she returned, she pointed it at the man's head and told him to "get off the facility and never come back." He refused to leave, which further upset Sherilyn. To scare him, she shot a few bullets at his feet, eventually forcing him. Does it sound like a charmer? He sounds like someone holding a grudge and trying to harm Jamison's, but when the FBI chased him and asked about his disappearance, he had a solid alibi and, as a suspect, Was excluded. Go figure

Disappearance of the Jamison family

October 16, 2009. According to Jamison's family and friends, it was not uncommon for them to disappear for days without really notifying anyone. Jamison often enjoyed loneliness and nature, often seeking out of reality. So no one was particularly worried when they weren't seen or heard for a few days. In addition to this, the family had informed Madison's school to pull her out when she moved, so the school did not ask after her.

Eight days after everyone last saw or heard from the Jamisons on the 8th, Hunter reported the abandoned truck at the top of Panorama Unten and reported it to police. The truck was locked and it seemed to have all of the family's possessions inside, including the dog Macy. Macy was miraculously still alive, but very malnourished by not eating anything for a few days. Authorities released Maysy from the truck and made him live with Bobby's mother.

Police have collected many personal items from trucks, such as cell phones, Sherilyn's wallets, and Bobby's wallets. Police believed that the family at the top of Panorama Unten should have been lost somewhere in the forest due to the incredibly dense trees and uneven terrain that made it difficult to move. Here, police used the GPS coordinates of Bobby and Sherilyn's mobile phones to map family movements. GPS climbed the hill and found a small footprint belonging to Madison.

When they arrived at the top of the hill, they found a photo on one of the cell phones taken in Madison. It's difficult to read her look in the photo. Opinions are somewhat divided regarding her feelings when the picture was taken. Some say she looks like she's laughing, while others say she's about to cry. Some believe that the photo wasn't taken by either of her parents, because she didn't smile in the photo and the way her arms were placed made her uncomfortable. I don't see this photo as particularly strong evidence, as it's pretty hard to tell what she's thinking from the photo. If she was afraid or threatened to take a picture, she would look horribly scared.

Police believed that the family spent about 15 minutes at the top of the mountain before returning to the truck. But since no one knows what happened after that, this is where the mystery really begins. Police conducted a large-scale search on the ground and helicopters, including search dogs, over 100 law enforcement agencies and the general public, on the 17th of the following day. But they couldn't find a family.

Police continued to search the truck for further clues about what had happened. In fact, they have found many promising prospects. Under the front seats of the truck was a bag with $32,000 in cash. They also found a very hostile and hatred 11-page long letter that Sherilyn wrote to Bobby. The letter stated that Sherilyn criticized Bobby as being a "hermit," feeling that Bobby did not care for his family and did not need them.

November 16, 2013

Bobby, Sherilyn, and Madison's bodies were found approximately three miles from where the truck was found. Now they are skeletons, and people immediately suspected that the body belonged to a family, which had to be confirmed by an Oklahoma health checker. In July 2014, the body was confirmed to be Jamison. However, they were so disassembled that the medical examiner was unable to identify the cause of death. However, Bobby was found to have a small hole behind the skull.

What happened to the Jamisons?

There are many theories about what happened to Jamison. Here we will discuss the most popular theories that appear over and over again.

So the best theory to start with is probably homicide suicide. Authorities began to seriously consider this when they discovered a long and hateful letter from Sherilyn to Bobby and an unstable episode caused by bipolar disorder. Another very concerned thing was that Sheriline was known to always carry a 0.22 pistol. However, when the police searched, there were no traces of a pistol on the truck. I couldn't find it anywhere in the house. But what if the gun was suicide suicide? It was not found near the body when they were found. Jamison's friends and family were against this theory, and the marriage of Sherilyn and Bobby was nervous, but they really love each other and Sherilyn could never do it to her family. I admit.

Friends and family, especially Niki, a friend of Sherilyn, supports the idea that Jamison was kidnapped. This could suggest that Jamison was struck by a gun and moved away from the truck, as there were no signs of any kind of struggle around the truck. This theory supports the fact that Jamison left all his belongings in the car. The fact that Jamison left his cell phone and wallet on the truck suggests that he might have been forced to leave the truck in a hurry due to lack of time to collect his luggage. I think this is quite likely in practice. Most of the time, considering that people take their cellphones and money with them everywhere, regardless of their lost plans.

Jamison installed a surveillance camera in front of the house Bobby's mother had installed. The reason for this, as Bobby's mother explained, was that she, Bobby, and Sherilyn were being threatened by Bobby's father, Bob. He appears to have been involved in drugs, gang activity and other sketchy things. Bobby filed a protection order against his father to protect him and his family. However, Bobby's father was actually in a nursing home at the time of his disappearance...I suspect he was personally linked to his disappearance, after all.

Surveillance cameras were used to record people who might have tried to enter the house. Investigators watched a video recorded from the day Jamison's disappearance found a video of Jamison packing a truck, perhaps in a "trans-like state." This was intriguing because Bobby and Sherilyn traveled back and forth between homes, often moving the boxes back and forth. Nor did they talk to or acknowledge each other while packing the truck. This wondered if people were "trans-like" to be drug-induced, in this case a stimulant, given how prevalent the drug is in this region. I always thought that Metz made people hyperactive, stimulating and aggressive. This is in contrast to how Jamison behaves in the video...

$32,000 cash again causes drug problems. Was money part of a terribly wrong drug trade and led to the killing of a family member? Again, I think it's a plausible theory. Jamison's friends and family said he wasn't involved in the drug, but who really knew them really well, given how private the family was?

There is also a suggestion that the Jamisons might have been involved in the cult, or might have planned to move to the area to join the cult, but when they got there, they were probably of some sort of cult ritual. I was a victim.

It's all very strange, and it feels like I don't know exactly what happened to Jamison. Did anyone really know them? I think they had far more to share with their family and friends than ever before. Perhaps if they were more open, their lives wouldn't end in that terribly mysterious way. Again, I don't know. I loved studying and writing about this case. If anyone has any ideas or theories about what happened, shoot them in my way!

10 THE MURDER OF LYNSEY QUY

In mid-December 1998, Lynsey Quy was missing from her home in Southport, England. It was 18 months ago that an investigator discovered that her husband, Mitchell Qui, had brutally killed her, disassembled her, and hid her body parts at various locations around Southport.

I hadn't heard about this a week ago, but when I heard it from a friend, it was very intriguing. As far as I know, it has never really been properly considered before, so I wanted to write about it. It is also interesting to consider the case where there is no existing opinion. I do my best here to tell the story of Lindsey, and I hope it is justice.

Lindsey was a shining person inside and out. She showed a beautiful, matching personality and a dazzling smile. Her mother, Linda, described her as cheerful, affectionate, and sociable. Lindsey came from a large family including her parents and her five brothers. The families were less intimate, but they love one another. When Lindsey became pregnant with her first serious boyfriend at the age of 17, she insisted on having a baby. But a few months after her pregnancy, the relationship ended and Lindsey was alone and 5 months pregnant.

Enter Mitchell Qui, who was three years older than Lindsey. At their first meeting, Mitchell quickly lost to Lindsey, but Lindsey thought she had beaten her. Mitchell was charming, always scattered around her, and came by her house with flowers and cards. Given Lindsey's pregnancy, she was particularly fascinated by the idea of dating and Mitchell looked perfect. Only five weeks later, the two were married.

But Lindsey's family wasn't so excited. It was so fast, did Lindsey really know Mitchell well? The two had already claimed, as remembered by

Lindsey's father, Peter, on their wedding night. "Maybe it was a sign to come," he said.

Another side of Mitchell

Soon Lindsey began to discover Mitchell's side of which she knew nothing. And he found that the man she married was a stranger. They found their first home together, but everything wasn't good. Lindsey told Mitchell to leave and confessed to her sister that Mitchell would often have a violent blast. Lindsey re-conceived Mitchell's child just one year after giving birth to her first child, Robin. Lindsey had an abortion in fear of bringing a new baby to an unstable home. This is a furious Mitchell who beat her and left.

In addition to being violent, Mitchell slept with other women on a regular basis while Lindsey and Lindsey were married. But after five months away, Lindsey allowed Mitchell to return. Due to a change of heart, she told Mitchell that she wanted to have a baby with him. Shortly after she got pregnant again.

Mitchell was still causing his most violent violence when Lindsey was almost half way pregnant. Lindsey wasn't home at the time, but the home seems confused when she returns. There were shards of glass everywhere, doors were not open, and blood was smearing the walls. The two were expelled from their homes and the marriage was once again in turmoil. In October 1997, their son Jack was born. But by the following year, Mitchell had moved again. This time it looked like it was gone forever.

Last forgiveness

With the help of women's help, Lindsey moved the children away from Mitchell and moved to another house. He was not informed of the location of his new home. Lindsey was so scary that she found Mitchell to have a portable panic button. Mitchell persuaded Jack to meet on his first birthday, as if he had just regained his life. From there, he will find a way back to Lindsey's house and her life. Lindsey didn't tell anyone that Mitchell and she were back together. When her friends and family knew, they were shocked that Lindsey allowed the man to return to her life and avoided them. Bringing Mitchell back was the worst decision Lindsay has ever made.

As Christmas approaches, Lindsey prepares her home for the festive season. On December 11, she spent time with her family, and at the end of the day her mother went home. Little did she know, this will be the last time she sees her daughter.

Lindsay disappears

The last time I saw Lindsey was on December 15, 1998. After that, there was no one to see or hear her again. On the 24th, Lindsey's mother tried to contact Lindsey throughout the day, asking when she could return Christmas gifts to her children. Needless to say, she didn't get in touch.

Lindsey was not actually reported missing until February 5, 1999, 53 days after someone last saw her. She was not reported missing by Mitchell or her family, but by a concerned social worker. After all, Lindsey was completely alone.

During the eighteen months that Lindsey was missing, Mitchell protected the public facade of her filthy husband, who was left behind to take care of her two young children, and his wife fled with another man. Did. No one who knew Lindsey believed this. She never chose to leave her children. Mitchell claimed several times that he had seen Lindsey, walked the streets, and drove Mercedes. But only he claimed to have seen him.

Lies and lies

Enjoying public relations, he told the media his story when he had the opportunity. He invited journalists to his home and meticulously built the web of lies. Mitchell has always been a mystery to journalists. When asked if they killed Lindsey, instead of answering "no", "I'm not going to answer that question, because I don't have to." Eventually everyone will know Because

Mitchell toys with the police, sending chief investigators in the case, Jeff Sloan, a Christmas card, and a bottle of hair dye, claiming to "cover his gray and give him more confidence." Such behavior confirmed how relaxed Mitchell was. He certainly did not come across because his husband was worried about his wife's welfare.

Whenever Mitchell appeared on TV, you never met him as a poor man. I was obviously uncomfortable to see him speak. He ran into a dishonesty when Lindsay went home and asked him to always grin as if he was sharing a private joke with him.

Meanwhile, Lindsey's family was in the dark. They knew Mitchell was guilty, did not trust him and knew how violent Mitchell was, but the lack of evidence could not condemn Mitchell .. While Lindsay was missing, they regularly exited into and around Southport looking for signs of Lindsey's body.

Mitchell's mask collapses
Mitchell thought he had successfully deceived the police, the public and Lindsey's family. For almost a year and a half, there were no signs of Lindsay. Investigators began to lose hope that they didn't want to know what had happened. When Mitchell muttered about how his life was essentially ruined by media reports (despite the fact that he did nothing to discourage it), the truth was finally about to come out. On June 7, 2000, police came to the conclusion that Lindsey died on or shortly after December 15, 1998. They went to Mitchell's house and brought him in for questioning. Mitchell didn't give up for about a day and a half, but he couldn't receive any more information on the evening of June 8. He confessed to all.

The next day, Mitchell agreed to show police where Lindsey was hiding the body. Mitchell kept smiling. Even after knowing that the media was there and finding him guilty for everyone, what seemed to him most importantly came into the limelight. That day, he showed the police hiding her torso and legs. Her head will never recover.

On December 16, 1998, Lindsey finally awakened to end Mitchell forever. She didn't mean to, but told Mitchell that she wanted to divorce and arranged an interview with a lawyer. Mitchell was furious. He strangled Lindsey and hid her body in the bedroom. With the help of his brother Elliot, he later dismantled her and disposed of a part of her body.

Mitchell was found guilty of one murder and sentenced to imprisonment. His brother was sentenced to seven years in prison for his role. Mitchell was named "The Killer of Smiles" because he was smiling during the search for Lindsey and all the while smiling until the police showed him various Lindsey cemeteries.

There is really something wrong with the judicial system when the perpetrators of such violent crimes may actually be free. Earlier this year, after serving a minimum sentence of 17 years, Mitchell was eligible for parole. He applied and was rejected, but he can apply for it at the same time next year as well. A petition was made to place Mitchell behind the prison. Lindsey's father says that every time he hears a prisoner commit suicide, he wants it to be Mitchell.

I can't say anything now, except I hope Lindsey is finally at peace. She really shone while she was alive, and I hope those who love her can remember her that way.

11 THE FREEWAY PHANTOM MURDERS

Between April 1971 and September 1972, Washington DC was terrified by a serial killer known to date only as the Freeway Phantom. In general, Freeway Phantoms brutally raped and killed six girls between the ages of 10 and 18.

This was the first serial killer I've covered here, and I wanted to go to something a little different that practically doesn't know anything. In fact, nobody seems familiar with this case. Is there a reason for this? Many at the time said that this was because the victim was a black man. It's still something that happens regularly, almost 50 years later.

victim
The first victim of Freeway Phantom was a 13-year-old Carol Spinks who was abducted on the way to the store in April 1971. Her body was found to be dumped beside the freeway six days later. She was raped and strangled and killed.

A second victim was found in early July, about six weeks later. On the way to work was 16-year-old Darrenia Johnson. She was found in the immediate vicinity of the site where Carol Spinks's body was dumped. However, the body was so disassembled that the investigators could not identify the cause of death.

Just two weeks later, the killer attacked again. The victim was a 10-year-old Brenda Crockett who went to the store at the direction of her mother. This time it was a little different. Brenda made two phone calls while she was with the murderer. Her sister answered the first call. Brenda told her that she was picked up by a white man and was on her way home by taxi. But before her sister answered, Brenda said goodbye and hung up. Brenda's second phone call was answered by her mother's boyfriend. The boyfriend is now in a white man's house. When he tried to ask Brenda more questions, Brenda hung up like she was on the first call. It was the last time someone heard from Brenda. She was found by the side of the highway a few hours later. She was raped and strangled with a scarf.

The African-American community in Washington DC was frightened for obvious reasons. The killer's trick was clear. He kidnapped a young defenseless black girl. They usually go to work, go to stores, and do their normal daily routine. They were raped, strangled, and dumped at various locations along the sides of the highway.

Then, on October 1, the murderer made a fourth attack. The victim this time was Nenomoshia Yates, 12 years old, heading home from the grocery store when she was missing. Within hours, her body was found by the side of the highway. She was also raped and strangled. It was after this murder that the murderer became known as the "Freeway Phantom" given his elusiveness and choice of location to leave the body of the victim.

On November 15, another agency was discovered. Brenda Woodward was the oldest of the 18-year-old victims. It was evening this time, so it was dark when the murderer was hit. Brenda was having dinner with her friend. The last person to see her was at the bus house. Later, early on November 16, police again discovered the body by the side of the highway. This time, the murderer changed his tactics a bit. Brenda was raped, stabbed and strangled. Her hitman took off her jacket and put it on her body. A note was found in the coat pocket. It read:

I love the linguistics of forensic medicine, which is very attractive. There is a lot to analyze in this note. The term "Tantamount" is used by people with a relatively high level of education. But misspellings confuse me. This is not a common error that actually occurs. If you're in a hurry or are scared, and you're not focused on what you're writing, you'll make a mistake. However, upon examining the memo, FBI investigators came to the conclusion that the memo was written by Brenda himself and directed by her by the killer.

Brenda was supposedly known to have known her killer. Her handwriting was solid and the notes were punctuation marks. I'm not sure, but even if you know the murderer, you may be afraid that you were abducted and you wrote down such a memo. I also misspelled it because I was afraid that Brenda wrote the note. Probably because I was in a hurry, I was more likely to make a mistake. There are many ways for you to see it. Also the exclamation mark...does it have a kind of joke with him and makes you feel like you had a good time?

Then everything stopped. Investigators thought the murderer had been moved or arrested for another unrelated crime. I had to continue my life.

Just as the fear began to wear off, the hitman struck again. Ten months later, in September 1972, a truck driver found the body of Diane Williams by the freeway. She spent her last night with her boyfriend walking home to the bus stop. Diane was strangled and killed.

Investigation and suspect
In 1974, a task force was established to investigate this case. Due to the large size of the MTF, we were able to interview and interrogate a large number of suspects and follow up on the tips and leads they were sent. But their investigation did not come to a firm conclusion.

A gangster known for abducting and rape girls and women in the Washington, DC/Maryland area, Green Vegarapist was the most suspect along the side of the highway from the abducted area. It was The girls were also the same age as the victims of the phantom murder on the highway. Claims that one of the gang members sniped another gang member and gave him some extra information about the murder committed by the Freeway Phantom, indicating that his fellow gang members were involved. did. However, all information provided to the police was mentioned in the press. He denied being involved in the Freeway Phantom killing when police interviewed members of the accused gang. He was also able to offer the police an alibi like he did when the girls were missing

Just about the time of the killings, police also had others in their minds. During the killings, the Watergate incident and subsequent actions and investigations began in earnest. As Watergate gained public protest and media attention, the Freeway phantom murder was driven away, drawing little interest from citizens outside the area where the girls lived.

Race question

Despite the fact that the investigators worked hard to catch the Freeway Phantom, the victim's family and friends still wondered, "Would the girl be a white person have caught the murderer?" ..

This question arose when the family of the victims of Freeway Phantom witnessed the period investigators went to settle the murder of a girl of the same profile at the place where they lived with their age. Except for that, the girl was white. Often mentioned is the abduction and murder of Catherine and Shearrayon in 1975, snatched while shopping at Wheaton, Maryland. The bodies of Catherine and Sheila were not found, but police worked vigorously to catch their murderers. In 2015, after the ColdCase investigation team picked up the case, we were able to gather evidence to sue Lloyd Welch for the killing of two girls. Welch, a convicted sex offender, is already in prison and in 2017 he confessed to the murder.

In 1972, Tommy Musgrove joined police in Washington, DC. He strongly agreed with the idea that race played an important role in whether the case was resolved, and was quoted as saying:

"These black girls didn't mean anything to anyone — I'm talking at the police station. If they were white, they put more labor into it. There was no doubt about that."

Lost hope

It is very unlikely today that the Freeway Phantom murder case will be resolved. Records are not kept in order at the police station, and the evidence stored at that time was lost or stolen, so no forensic examination is currently possible. The terrible truth is that families probably do not see justice for their daughters, sisters, friends and neighbors. Fifty years later, they still wonder if something could be done in the dark to prevent the worst nightmare from becoming a reality.

12 THE DISAPPEARANCE
OF KYRON HORMAN

Friday June 4, 2010 wasn't just a day for the seven-year-old Chiron Hohmann. It was an annual science fair day when I was a sophomore at Skyline Elementary School in Portland, Oregon. Chiron was a science fan and was excited to attend the fair and learn about his alumni projects. He was particularly proud of his own project on the red-eyed tree frog.

Kayne's father, Kaine, had a chat with Chiron that morning and was planning to go to ice cream after school. Kane couldn't attend the fair because she had to go to work, but Chiron's stepmother Terry intended to take him. Kane loves him and talks to Chiron who watches him leave with Terry. Since then, Kane hasn't seen his son.

Chiron Hohmann

Chiron was born on September 9, 2002 in Desiree Davidson and Kane Hohmann, who worked as engineers at Intel. Desire and Kane divorced before Chiron was born, but the two shared custody. In 2004, Desiree became seriously ill with renal failure, had to spend a long time in the hospital, and was unable to properly care for Kyron. At this point, Kane had taken over full custody, but Desiree was as active as possible in his son's life.

In 2007, Kane married Terri Moulton, a primary school teacher in Roseburg, Oregon. Since Kane and Desiree were divorced, they have been together and Terry has raised Chiron like his son. Terry also had a teenage son, James, from her first marriage. Terry and Kane had daughter Chiara in December 2008. After giving birth to Chiara, Terry began to suffer postpartum depression. Around this time, Kane and Terry's marriage began to collapse.

Desire moved to Medford, about four and a half hours drive from Portland in southern Oregon (not sure). This meant she could not see Chiron as often as she wanted. She married Tony Young, a detective in Medford.

June 4, 2010 event
Terry, along with baby Chiara, took Chiron to the Science Fair as planned. At 8:15am, PTA School Principal Gina Zimmermann saw Chiron and Terry standing together next to the exhibit. Terry takes a picture of Chiron in his project and later posts it on Facebook.

At 8:45 am, Terry claimed she saw Chiron walking down the hallway towards the classroom. This aspect of the case is important. Many believe that Chiron left Terry instead of going to his classroom. However, there have been no reports of the two witnessing together since 8:45 am.

According to Terry, she then left school and started doing business, going to Fred Meyer's grocery store about seven miles away and buying Chiara's deaf ears medicine. She had a receipt at 9:12 AM indicating she bought something from the store, but they didn't have the medicine they needed, so they headed to another Fred Meyer. Surveillance footage showed her in both stores.

From 10:10 am, Terry claimed that after taking the drug, he spent about an hour and a half driving down a rural road in northwestern Multnomah County to put Kiara to sleep. I couldn't find the exact details, but I don't think she was driving all the time. I think she spent all her time on the phone sitting in the car while Kiara was sleeping. This alerted the investigators as no one could confirm Terry's whereabouts at this time.

Terri then headed to the fitness gym for 24 hours, entered at 11:39 am and left Kiara for an onsite daycare center. She was there for about 40 minutes, went home with Kiara at 12:20 pm and arrived about 20 minutes later.

At 1:21 pm, she uploaded to Facebook her photos taken by Chiron at the Science Fair. This includes photos related to the case, where Chiron was smiling in front of the Tree Frog project, wearing the glasses he always wore, a shirt with the black T-"CSI" logo and dark cargo pants. ..

Kane returned home at 2pm. Terry and Kane walked with Chiara at 3:30 pm to the bus stop in Chiron and picked him up as usual. However, the bus came and there was no sign of Chiron. The bus driver explained that Chiron had never boarded the bus and called on his school secretary to ask him where he was. The secretary reported that he was absent at 10 am when the class began that day. From that point on, the situation escalated rapidly. Kane and Terry rushed to school. At 3:45 pm, Chiron was reported missing.

Why didn't the school call someone when Chiron was marked absent?

Usually, if a child, especially an elementary school child, is marked absent, the child's parents will be notified immediately. But Chiron's teacher thought Terry had taken him to see a doctor. According to Terry, she told her teacher at the science fair that she was going to see another project with Chiron. Terry claimed that the teacher misunderstood her saying she was taking Chiron and Chiara to see a doctor. Terry was confused about how the teacher misunderstood her so much.

Terry informed the school that Chiron had a visit, so the doctor's visit request is not entirely unfounded, but the visit day seems confusing. Terry claimed:

"For the past two weeks, he's been acting really weird. Staring at the universe. I can't remember anything. Step into the room, then go back and stare, then proceed. The doctor said he had a small bout. I think he's waking up and I applied Thursday to check him out next Friday [June 11th]."

Meanwhile, sources from the school told police and the media that Terry notified the school that there was a doctor appointment in Chiron on June 4. It would also have been strange for Teri to inform the school of Chiron's appointment. June 11th because June 4th was the last day of school before summer vacation. There are many misunderstandings in this case.

Given that Chiron was not seen for about seven hours, when police were informed that he was missing, they responded promptly and immediately proceeded with organizing a large search.

Exploring Chiron – June 4 – June 14

At 4:33 pm, Portland Police and Police Officer Multnomah County Sheriff began arriving at Skyline Elementary School and Homan's House. At 5:30 pm, a quick broadcast message from Portland Public Schools was sent to the family in the school district, and the phone was informed that "Today Chiron

Hohmann did not go home."

The search involved 65 detectives, 60 trained searchers, and more volunteers, focusing on the school and the two-mile radius around it.

At 10:40 pm, police officers reported that they were searching through every corner of Skyline School, including all crawl spaces, storage locations, classrooms, and buildings. The Hohmann family was also searched. There were no signs of Chiron.

The search continued on weekends, involving search and rescue groups of independent experts. During a press conference, authorities announced that the FBI and the National Guard were involved in the investigation.

All Skyline Elementary students and staff were interrogated by criminals. Terri ordered posters for 1,000 missing people and distributed them throughout the region.

Allegations were raised by the public regarding the silence of the entire Chiron family. This prompted FBI spokespersons to issue the following statement:

The public did not respond well to this. It further strengthened their suspicions that the family was hiding something. Two days later, Chiron's family held a press conference with pressure from the masses and the media. Tony Young said: "We miss you, we love you and now you need to be at home."

Tony and Kaine thanked everyone in the community for their support and thank everyone involved in the search for Kyron. I didn't tell Terry or Desire.

On Friday, June 11, the Chiron search was expanded to include Sorby Island, about 6 miles from Skyline Elementary School. In this case, many consider Sobi to be red herring. Terry's phone seems to have pinged the towers of cell phones that serve not only Sobier Island but the wide area around the island. But Terry wasn't on the island that day. The Sorby Island Bridge has surveillance cameras that show all vehicles entering and leaving the island. The track Terry was driving wasn't included in the June 4 video, so I'm pretty sure she wasn't there. Anyway, the island has been extensively searched for horse, helicopter and diver searchers. They found no signs of

Chiron.

On Sunday, June 13, a press conference was held, ending a large-scale investigation of Chiron, and it was announced that the case was now a criminal investigation. The search, with more than 1300 participants, was the largest in Oregon history. A $25,000 reward was posted to everyone who could provide information about Kyron's whereabouts. By the end of July, the reward had doubled to £20,000.

Terry's secret...
About three weeks after Chiron disappeared, Terry's life began to run wild.

The day after Chiron's disappearance, it was discovered that Terry was texting and emailing friends about what happened that day. She writes: There was no man on the chaperone list.

Everyone else was completely focused on finding Chiron, but this was considered somewhat inappropriate as Terry texted and emailed friends. Bruce McCain, former captain of the Martonoma County Sheriff's Office, said:

"It's all about Terry, poor, poor Terry, not a single concern about Chiron. She keeps talking about Chaperon, who is already making Alivis, and about the appointment of a doctor.

I don't know the exact date, but between June 4th and June 25th, Terri ran two polygraph tests, both of which failed. She complained that she couldn't properly ask the question. She was surprised to discover she had failed and claimed to have told the truth.

On Saturday, June 26, Kane left Homan's house and took baby Chiara. Terri made two phone calls that day. The first was classified as a "blackmail" phone at 5:17 pm and the second was classified as a "child care" phone at 11:39 pm.

In early July, the media began reporting on shocking revelations. It explains Kane's reasons for his actions detailed above. A landscaper by the name of Rodolfo Sanchez, which Terry hired for gardening, reported to police that he met Terry at a restaurant about six months before Chiron's disappearance and offered him money to kill her husband.

According to Sanchez, Terry explained to him that Kane was physically and emotionally abusive and she was afraid to take away Chiara. Apparently she told him that Kaine always had $10,000 on his person (?!) and could kill him and look like a robbery. His reward was probably the $10,000 Kaine being carried. He also told authorities that he and Terry were having an affair.

This is an increase in Terry's guilt for many, but to be honest, I think it sounds quite humorous. Reddit user Smokin-Okie has created a nice detailed article about this case (see source link) and has made many holes in the Sanchez story. The biggest problem is that Sanchez does not speak fluent English and Terry does not speak fluent Spanish. For his deposit, he needed a translator so that all the questions he asked were translated into Spanish and all the answers he provided were translated into English. Another, if he and Terry had an affair, why she felt she had to ask her restaurant, public place with her baby daughter to ask her to kill her husband Is it? Didn't she do this when they were together?

In other words, it was June 26th. Police organized a sting operation. Sanchez went to Terry's door and handed her $10,000 or demanded that he go to the authorities for plans for his murder. An undercover agent monitored the vicinity and Sanchez wore wires. They assured that Kane wasn't home at that time. Terry was (of course) frightened and said nothing to Sanchez. She ran through the house and called 911. This was the "threat" phone mentioned above.

Despite the failure of the assassination operation and the lack of solid evidence, police considered Sanchez to be credible, notifying Kane that Terry had tried to kill him, and thereby suddenly left home with Chiara. It was Later that night, Terry called the aforementioned custody phone. On Monday, June 28, Terri was issued a ban and petition to end the marriage. The reasons for Kane requesting a restraint order are:

"I think the defendant was involved in the disappearance of his son, Chiron, who has been missing since June 4, and I learned that the defendant tried to hire someone to kill me. The police have provided me with reason to believe the above two statements.

Shortly after Terry's detention order and divorce petition, she began an affair with Kane's high school classmate Michael Cook. Terry and Cook began to spend time together, exchanging text messages and pictures of a sexual nature.

A court document was filed on Monday, July 12, and Kane accused Terry of violating a detained binding order by allowing Terry to show Cook and take pictures. He also claimed Terry tried to kidnap Kiara from Jim's Day Care Center during his workout. For these reasons Terry was required to be insulted in court.

On July 16, Terry agreed to move from a house he did not share with Kaine, Chiron and Chiara. She stayed with her parents and Kane and Chiara returned to their Portland home.

Further inquiries to the police
Police began to focus on Terry's friend, DeDe Spicher, to see if they could provide further information about the day Chiron disappeared, or perhaps even the accomplice of Chiron's disappearance. Keep in mind that while police are thoroughly investigating Terry, they have never officially nominated her as a suspect.

DeDe moved in with Terri for 11 days after Terri was arrested by Kaine. In mid-July, police searched DeDe's home and asked her about her move on the day Chiron disappeared. When asked, DeDe informed police that he was doing gardening all day in a house in northwestern Portland. However, contrary to DeDe's story, the homeowner stepped forward and informed the police that DeDe had suddenly left at 11:30 am and did not return until around 1 pm. They also tried to call DeDe in the meantime, but there was no response. This caused police to suspect DeDe, who decided to locate her in 90 minutes, when she was unexplained.

On Monday, July 26, DeDe was summoned to testify before a grand jury in Multnomah County investigated the Chiron's disappearance. Last Friday, Kaine Horman and Desiree Young issued a statement showing distrust of DeDe.

"She is in close contact with Terry and has provided Terry with support and advice that is not in the best interest of our son."

They said she wasn't cooperating with the investigation, clearly "suggesting others not to cooperate with the investigation to others who might have information about Chiron's disappearance."

Dede's lawyer Chad Stavley disagreed with the statement, saying his client was "extremely supportive" in the investigation, investigating her home and car, and responding to a few hours of criminal interrogation.

Dede interviewed People magazine. During the interview, she expressed her belief in Terry's innocence.

"During all these years as her friend, something that leads me to believe that she is in some way or motivated to do something like this I have never seen it."

She added:

"I have this fear my friends are experiencing," she said. "I wouldn't have been there if she thought she could do a [foul]. She wouldn't have been my friend in the first place."

truck
On August 11, police held a press conference requesting information about Terri's Ford F-250 pickup truck she was driving, suing Kyron on the day of her missing. They said another adult was sitting in the truck and two witnesses came out in front.

Given that this person could possibly be DeDe, give us a copy of the Terri, DeDe, and truck pictures in the flyer, and anyone who has the information should come. Investigators were particularly interested in the sightings that occurred between 9:45 am and 1:00 pm. Their interest in sighting was not limited to DeDe. They were looking for explanations of other adults who appear to be in the truck or left near the truck.

However, on August 18, Portland News Station Kathu 2 reported that there was reason to believe there might have been no DeDe on the track that day.

My thoughts

I think someone took Chiron, perhaps someone he trusted, or someone who could gain his trust, for example someone who told him he knew his mother or father. Perhaps they could lure him into the front of the school and into the car.

In the first interview with Terry after Chiron's disappearance, she described Chiron as "not a real adventurer" and "a little timid," and couldn't imagine him just wandering himself. Terry is the only person considered to be interested in Chiron's disappearance. This is understandable because she was the last person to report meeting him on the day he left. When people first read about this case, I think it's easy to focus on Terry and conclude that she must be guilty.

But the more I investigated the case, the more I doubted these assumptions of Terry's guilt. In my opinion, I outline some of the reasons for and against Terri's guilt. This is based solely on my own research and analysis.

for

Terry was the last person to see Chiron that day, claiming she saw him walking down the hallway towards the classroom. No one claimed to have met him at that time, nor was there any report of his sightings after this. It's very strange that a school full of adults and kids (which would have been busier than usual given the science fair) did not support her claim.

According to Terry's friend, she moved her son, James, from home in February 2010, leaving Kane angry for several months before her disappearance in Chiron. .. Kane and James did not get along, often argued, and Kane felt that he was causing tension at home, causing unnecessary stress on Terry and did not help her with depression. One of the less persuasive theories is that Terry was angry with Kaine and wanted to harm Chiron and go back to him. This could be part of a combination of reasons why Terry harms Chiron and is probably combined with her depression, but I can't imagine it's the soul reason she wants Chiron erased.

Desiree Young always believes that Terry is involved in his son's disappearance and is convinced that Terry planned everything. She promised Terry to "do the right thing" to move forward. In June 2012, Desiree filed a civil suit against Terri in order to prove that Terri kidnapped her son and knew of his whereabouts. She asked Terry for $10 million in damages. But a year later, the lawsuit was dropped and Desire explained that he did not want to interfere with the investigation. Digiry told the media in the months leading up to her son's disappearance:

   "Chiron was getting more and more frustrated about not spending time with me. He wanted to live with us. He broke several times and just wanted to stay I sobbed."

Against

The claim that nobody has ever seen Chiron walking down the corridor also turns into Terry's favor. Now, except Terry, no one saw Chiron in the hall. Also, nobody saw Chiron with Terry after 8:45 am. The science fair they left shortly before 8:45 am was the last report the two witnessed together. People could have seen them later, but Terry and Chiron naturally saw them together, so we didn't think about anything. But I don't think this is the case. In this case, focusing on Terry, they would have reported sightings if anyone saw Chiron with her at any time after 8:45 am. But no one has it.

What I thought was a little weird was Kane's complete redirection in his opinion of Terry. A few weeks after Chiron disappeared, he said about Terry:

"I think she, like other families, is committed to finding Chiron."

It's only natural that Terry suddenly was told by police that he was trying to kill him and completely ate him, and he understood why he and Chiara left because of their warning that they could be at risk. can. But at the same time, he seemed completely convinced that Terry was responsible for Chiron's disappearance. This could be due to a polygraph test that Terry failed. I think Kane's reaction to the conspiracy to hire and kill was similar to the general reaction, such as "what else can this woman do to hire someone to kill her husband?". But, as I explained before, I think the whole story of a murder plan for employment is very dubious and honestly it can be composed, and Rodolfo Sanchez does it for the sake of caution. did.

Conclusion

My idea about this case is that everything that Terry did or didn't do really clouded the water and was distracted by Chiron's disappearance. I think the public didn't like her from the beginning and she got a bad mood from her and she was easy to point her finger at.

I admit that this case was so important that it was sometimes difficult to stitch information together to make my conclusion. I'm not sure about Terry's guilt. I don't think she's a great moral person, but I don't think this made her a kidnapper/murderer. Maybe I will get a lot of sticks for this. From what I can tell, most people believe she is guilty.

The really sad thing about this case is that Chiron did not always seem to be the main focus. In my research, there was no doubt that the media focused on Terry's personal life (her friend, her case, her scandal) rather than the fact that a little boy was missing.

In June 2019, Chiron will be missing for nine years. Kane and Desiree believe that he is still alive, but of course, as days go by, it becomes increasingly difficult to keep hope. The investigation of Chiron is ongoing and investigators say the case is still pending and active.

I can't even imagine how hard this would be for everyone who loves Chiron, especially Kane and Desiree. Hope someday they will get the answers they deserve.

"I'm still expecting to receive the call I'm waiting for, you know the call,'Desilly, this is the police, we found Chiron,'" she wrote. .. "I want the phone above all else, I want to see the police standing in front of me waiting to say I found him. I grabbed Chiron a second time and held him until he said Mum dreaming of a day to hug, can't breathe, overcame that moment and planned in detail in my head, dreaming about it many times before it became a dream.- Desiree Young.

13 THE CHICAGO TYLENOL POISONINGS

When you wake up, your head pounds, you are enthusiastic, and your whole body hurts. There is no doubt that the latest working bugs have come through your family/friends/colleagues and have finally come to you. You feel quite miserable, but not as distressing as visiting a doctor. So you force yourself out of bed, go to the medicine cabinet, and pop a couple of painkillers. It's very easy. Maybe this is just an overdose and you will feel better at the end of the day. However, if you do not take it, you will take the drug every 4 hours. Until you start feeling yourself again.

The rise of Tylenol

Tylenol is the trade name for acetaminophen, the most common OTC analgesic in the United States. In the UK, acetaminophen is most commonly called paracetamol. Johnson & Johnson is the parent company of McNeil Consumer Products, the manufacturer of Tylenol. McNeill first established the brand Tylenol in 1955.

By September 1982, Tylenol sales had grown rapidly, accounting for 35% of the OTC analgesic market. Market share% was estimated to continue to grow from the rest of the year to the next year.

Bitter pill to swallow

However, this growth did not continue because something unexpected happened. In many words, it was a disaster for both Tylenol consumers and distributors. On September 29 and a few days later, ingestion of Tylenol with cyanide resulted in the deaths of seven people living in and around Chicago. On the morning of September 30, I found out that a terrible thing happened in Johnson and Johnson. Over the next few weeks, Tylenol's market share plunged from 35% to 8%.

victim

The first death that occurred as a result of the addiction was 12-year-old Mary Kellerman in Elk Grove Village outside Chicago. On the morning of September 29th, Mary woke up pretty wild. She had a fever, had a headache, and had a sore throat. Her parents decided to keep her house away from school that day. They gave her extra power Tylenol and she returned to bed. By 7am that morning, Mary was dead.

The same day, 27-year-old Adam Janus, working at the post office, further strengthened Tylenol. He died later in the day in hospital from what was originally thought to be a major heart attack.

Shocked by his brother's death, 25-year-old Stanley Janus returned home with his wife, 19-year-old Teresayanus. Stanley and Teresa both tried to comfort and embrace the upset family, but both had headaches, each strengthening Tylenol from Adam's bottle. Both were taken to the hospital, Stanley died later that day, and Teresa died a few days later. During the 48 hours, three of the Janus family died unexpectedly. The Janus family and the authorities were completely perplexed by a mysterious tragedy.

The following day, three more mysterious deaths occurred. This includes 31-year-old Mary McFarland of Elmhurst, Illinois, Chicago's 35-year-old Paula Prince, and Winfield's 27-year-old Mary Liner.

Early investigation

The most obvious place to start the investigation was three members of the Janus family. Talking with their families about their deaths, investigators discovered that each was drinking strong Tylenol capsules shortly before they died. Then it turns out that 12-year-old Mary Kellerman did the same.

Various sources generally trust "investigators" for discovering that Tylenol was killing people. We also found sources that claimed to be the nurse Helen Jensen, who made this discovery first.

Police took a bottle of Tylenol as evidence from Kellerman and Janus families. When confiscating and inspecting the bottle, the investigators worked with Dr. Edmund Donohue, a physician in Cook County, explaining that potassium cyanide has an almond flavor. They sniffed the bottles and what they guessed... they smelled like almonds.

The lot numbers for the two Tylenol bottles indicate they were produced as part of the same batch, but are made at different plants in very remote areas of the country. The investigators have concluded that tampering at the manufacturing level is almost impossible. It wouldn't work at all if the tablets were poisoned on the other side of the country and all ended up inside and outside Chicago. Therefore, it was determined that tampering would occur when the bottle arrived on the store shelves. Johnson and Johnson told consumers that this is the case.

What's wrong?

It is believed that the criminal traveled around the various convenience store/grocery stores where Tylenol was sold, picked a few bottles, and carried them from the store.

They opened a jar of tablets that had no means of being tampered with and took out some tablets. The tablets had a typical capsule design. Therefore, they opened them, dumped the drug and replaced it with cyanide. They also did not shed light on cyanide. They literally filled the capsule. Blood test results of the victims showed that they had a lethal dose of cyanide in their system of 100-1000x.

Johnson and Johnson's response

The reaction of Johnson and Johnson's products to tampering is hailed as one of the company's best responses to a disaster of this magnitude. They recalled more than 31 million Tylenol bottles nationwide (retail price over $100 million), notified consumers to dispose of bottles they had already purchased, and refunded them. The hospital was also instructed to dispose of the Tylenol capsules it had at hand. Next, Johnson and Johnson continued to offer a $100,000 award for information that could lead to the perpetrator.

We tested 1.5 million bottles and found that 10 bottles contained poisons. Some bottles contained 3-4 poisons, while others contained more than 6. No bottle was discarded by the consumer in the test, so no one knew exactly how many bottles the poisoned tablet contained.

Suspect

Who did it? why? No one knows.

Here are the most commonly suspected cases of my research.

Number One: James Lewis, Tax Accountant
The most popular suspect in this case. Lewis is a really strange man. He seemed to like to play with the investigator, but he never pulled it away. In the weeks following the death of the poisoning, Johnson and Johnson received a letter from Lewis demanding "stop the kill" by wiring $ 1,000,000 to a bank account. Then he will probably tell them where to find the poison.

Johnson and Johnson didn't want that-they immediately turned the letter into an FBI and found the fingerprint of the letter and led them to Lewis. Lewis lived in a short-term hotel in New York at the time. Throughout the interrogation, Lewis remained guilty and guilty, but was imprisoned for 20 years for extortion. While in prison, Lewis continued to write an investigator about his thoughts on the case. He seemed reasonably aware in these letters detailing how to inject cyanide into Tylenol capsules. Lewis was released on parole after spending 13 years in prison. Since his release, Lewis has written novels about randomly poisoned people in Chicago. Very strange.

His work in Boston was attacked by the FBI in 2009, given the ongoing investigation into Tylenol addiction and Lewis being the most likely suspect. They took a DNA sample and confiscated his computer, but couldn't charge him because he couldn't be placed in the right place at the right time.

Number 2: Ted Kazinski (aka). Unbombed
There was never much real evidence pointing to Kachinsky in Tylenol addiction. The bombing by Kachinsky was a domestic terrorist act as well as Tylenol addiction. In Kaczynski's manifesto "Industrial Society and the Future", we write about technology giants taking over people's lives and polluting the environment.

The main reason Kazinski was considered a suspected addiction was that he was from the Chicago area and his first bombing targeted people from Chicago to the surrounding areas. The presidents of DC and United Airlines lived in Lake Forest, Illinois. Kachinsky's parents also lived in Lombard, Illinois, on the outskirts of Chicago, where Kachinsky occasionally stayed.

In 2011, investigators obtained a DNA sample from Kaczynski, but found nothing to connect him to Tylenol addiction. Throughout, Kazinski denied having owned cyanide. Kacinski, now 76, was sentenced to eight consecutive life sentences, with no possibility of parole on the bomb, killing three and injuring many others.

Number 3: Roger Arnold

Arnold was an employee of a gem supermarket distribution center. Tyrrenol was sold at a Jewel supermarket, so Roger would have been handling it on a regular basis. One night at the bar, Arnold was talking about killing people with cyanide. Someone in jail reported this to police who questioned Arnold for three days. They made him go because they found no evidence that he was involved in Tylenol addiction. Returning to the bar a few weeks later, Arnold lost it and shot deadly a man who believed he had reported him to the police (who had nothing to do with him, who I didn't know if there was one). Arnold was sentenced to 30 years in prison, but was released on parole 15 years later. Arnold died in 2008.

Imitation?

They urged many other crap to follow their example, as if this man didn't smoke enough. In the month following the first Tylenol poisoning, more than 270 cases were reported of product tampering. These usually contain OTC drugs such as Tylenol, which are contaminated with something not made for human consumption. The victim was usually his spouse. In 1986, Stella Nickel, Auburn, WA, incorporated cyanide into Exedrine tablets to poison her husband. She put poisoned Exedrin back on the shelves of the store to hide her tracks, leading to the death of a stranger, Susan Snow. However, nickel was less familiar than the original Tylenol addict. She was arrested and charged with two deaths. Currently she is serving 90 years in prison. This year, 2018 is the first year Nickell is on parole, but I haven't found any updates on this yet.

New packaging regulations

Did you know that today's medications are not so easy to actually open the body? There's a reason: Chicago Tylenol Addiction!

In response to the addiction directly, McNeill introduced a safe sealed tamper proof package.

Johnson and Johnson later removed the capsule as a delivery form of

Tylenol because the capsule was easily opened and contaminated, as happened in Chicago in 1982. They have released a solid "gel caplet" that cannot be opened and reassembled as a capsule. Can be.

In 1983, tampering with the product became a federal crime, as was Tylenol. This is called the "Federal Tamper Prevention Bill" or the "Tylenol Bill."

To date, the Tylenol murder remains unresolved. There are multiple suspects, but none have been convicted of murder. The case is still under investigation, but given that the murder occurred more than 36 years ago, there are now few leads on who committed them.

Personally, I didn't have to work very hard on the bottle seals or pop the painkiller under the foil. It has been tampered with." I always grew up watching it, so I didn't know anything different. Now, it's really strange to think that once in a time of innocence, the product didn't have the protection it has today. I think it's really really sad because the bad guys took to understand the need for these protections by killing a bunch of strangers...why people are just nice and hurt each other. Isn't it not? But if it is necessary to keep people safe, then so.

14 THE DEATH OF MITRICE RICHARDSON

In the last few weeks there has been a lot of debate in the US over the slogan "Defund the Police." I sincerely agree with the movement proposing to divert funds from the police department to other departments that can better promote and achieve public safety such as social services. Let's face it- American police stations are ridiculously over-funded. The United States is not a war-torn country, but it is easy to make mistakes because policemen roam around with grenade launchers, high-performance assault weapons, and armored tanks running around Main Street.

However, I don't like the slogan "Defund the Police". It requires a lot of explanation and provides too much feed to those who are intentionally intended to confuse and mislead the public for political gain. In my opinion, we need a new name that reduces our vulnerability to these malicious attacks.

The stats that only 5% of US police calls are reports of violent crimes is amazing as I have encountered several times in the last few weeks. The remaining 95% of calls are made to report relatively benign incidents, such as noise complaints, trespassing, and illegal sales of goods (eg, cigarettes that led police to kill Eric Garner). It was.

95% of the reports are from people with mental health problems such as bipolar episodes. Mental health and policing topics are central to the cases we are about to discuss. The very sad reality is that the victims of this case, Mitrice Richardson, would probably still be alive today, even if the American people did not rely heavily on police to solve all the problems. Mitrice is a classic example of why the public needs to call a non-police option (not trained as a mental health professional) if they are concerned about their personal health.

Mitrice Richardson was born on April 30, 1985, in Latice Sutton and Michael Richardson, Covina, California. Michael and Lattice divorced when Mitrice was very young, and Lattice married Larry Sutton, Mitris's stepfather. Michael spent his childhood in prison (I don't know what it was), but after being released, looked back on his life and immersed himself in his career in the medical industry. Michael didn't play much of a role in raising his daughter, but as she grew older, he and Mitrice got closer.

Smart, cute, thoughtful, and kind Mitrice was the type of person everyone wanted to be friends with. In 2008, he graduated from California State University Fullerton with a bachelor's degree in psychology. An honor student who consistently achieved 4.0 GPA, Mitrice was eager to enter graduate school. She began her internship at the office of clinical psychologist and family best friend Ronda Hampton. At this point, she lived in her great-grandmother Mildred Hughes and South LA, working as a go-go dancer at a local nightclub to save money. She also participated in a beauty contest and did modeling.

Mitrice's life changes
In the fall of 2009, Mitrice started showing signs that something was wrong. She recently broke up with her two-year-old girlfriend, Tessa Moon, but it was not only the sadness caused by the farewell that caused Mitrice's behavioral changes.

Mitrice had bipolar disorder. It is not clear when it was diagnosed, but by that time she seemed to control it. Latice began receiving weird texts from her daughter, and she began posting something extraordinary on her social media profile. In one of her last Facebook posts, she wrote:

Worried, Latice tried to contact Mitrice several times, but didn't answer the phone.

The last meal of Mitrique
On Wednesday, September 16, 2009, Mitrice voluntarily drove from her great-grandmother's house to Malibu in South LA and arrived around dinner. The drive is about 40 miles along a series of winding cliff roads. She drove to Jeffreys, one of the many fine restaurants in Malibu, got out of the car and approached the clerk. The clerk immediately got the impression that something was going up. Mitrice behaved crazy and was talking about

"Revenge of the Death of Michael Jackson." The clerk got into her car and parked, thinking she might be just an outlander. When he returned, he found Mitlis running in his glove box in his car (which he had left open). He asked her if she was okay and if he would get out of his car. She followed and walked to the restaurant.

Mitrice approached a regular customer table at another restaurant and invited him to sit with him. For example, he made a strange statement that he was from Mars. She wasn't threatened and they weren't too worried about disturbing dinner so others were playing with them at the table. Mitrice ordered Kobe Steak and Ocean Breeze Cocktail. Her bill came to $89, but she couldn't pay. This is a bit vague-it's not clear if she refused to pay or couldn't pay because she didn't have a wallet in her car (but if she left it, why she It's unclear if he just didn't go out in her car to get it).

The restaurant is as responsive as possible, so I asked if I could call someone to pay for my meal. Mitrice only remembered Mildred's (her great-grandmother) number. Mildred suggested paying over the phone, but the restaurant needed a fax signature. Mildred didn't have a fax machine.

The police are called
At a loss, Jeffries' manager called the police. According to the LA Times, he was worried about her welfare. He reasoned that she would be kept safer than going out on her own. "He wanted them to get in touch with her family and help her get home safely."

(This was a model situation to call a mental health professional instead of police if such services were available. Unfortunately, such an option is not available to restaurant managers. No, it doesn't exist until today.)

This is where things get cluttered. The following event shows how the sheriff department handled everything well. About 9 pm, three Los Angeles County Security Department (LASD) agents were dispatched to Jeffreys. They had the impression that Mitrice was drunk or taking drugs-the restaurant manager told the dispatcher she was "a bit euphoric and a bit weird". When they arrived, they exhaled her and she passed the drinking test. They were supposed to arrest Mitrice on charges of "inn owner fraud" and possession of marijuana (they found less than an ounce in her car). They may have taken her for a psychiatric assessment, but she seems to have been arrested because it was a "simpler option." The restaurant did not prosecute Mitrice for not paying her bills.

Mitrice's car contained all my personal belongings, including my phone, wallet, and ATM card. The agent drove her to the Malibu/Lost Hills Sheriff's station, about 20 minutes north of Malibu, and she was booked at 11:00 pm. According to the station's logbook, Mitrice called four times while in detention. She told the deputies that she was her great-grandmother, but the call was not recorded due to a recording device malfunction. Oddly enough is that her great-grandmother claimed she didn't receive a phone call from Mitrise that night, and the phone company didn't show her phone records.

Mitrice's mother, Latice, knew what had happened and called the station to ask if he would detain Mitrice at night or release her. If they planned to release her, she would pick her up, according to Mr. Lattes. If they did not plan to release her, she would come in the morning and pick her up. It was midnight, and the drive from Covina to Lost Hills Station is about 50 minutes. She also had her second daughter at home. Latex made a warning joke with his deputy prime minister over the phone.

The Deputy Prime Minister has repeatedly warned Latice to detain his daughters and release them in the morning. Latice was pleased with Mitrice's safety, thanked the deputy and hung up around 12:30 am.

Mitrice has been released

Approximately five minutes after the call ended, Mitrice was released from detention, as opposed to the Deputy Secretary calling Latice over the phone. She was told that she could sleep in the lobby and wait for her mother to pick up in the morning. But keep in mind, whatever the officer says, Mitrice didn't have a healthy mind at that time. She was free to leave, and that's exactly what she did-security footage shows her discharged and leaving the station. However, the footage went "missing" for several months and was eventually found in the desk drawer of Sheriff Captain Thomas Martin.

It's midnight and there's no Lost Hills train station anywhere. Mitrice didn't even have a wallet, phone, or even a jacket, so he began to walk the way to the station to the Santa Monica Mountains. Moving in the dark is dangerous and nearly impossible. According to Google Maps, it takes 6 hours to walk 16 miles in the mountains back to Malibu (assuming the lights were off, I had the proper equipment and knew where to go). No one knew where to go when Mitrice disappeared at night, but she had never arrived at her destination.

At 5:30 am the next day, Lattice called the station and asked about Mitrise's ride, but she was informed that she had been released and departed. Latex was naturally upset that she was lying. Assembling herself, she asked the vice over the phone how she could submit the missing person's report. But her concerns were filled with indifference and told that she wasn't long enough to submit (she was told to wait 24 hours).

I received some promising information from a man named Bill Smith, the former reporter of KTLA News. A former reporter at KTLA News called on police to report wandering the woman early that morning (probably around 6:30 am, about 6 hours after the release of Mitlis). About 6 miles west of Lost Hills Station, Smith's residence was at the bottom of the dark canyon of the gated community. Smith described her as "a slim black woman with Afro hair". Smith reported that he called from his window to ask if he was okay, and replied to her "just resting." By the time Smith wore something out for him to go out and investigate, she disappeared into the mountains across the house.

Failed investigation
From the beginning, Sheriff's Office had completely mismanaged the investigation into Matrice Richardson's disappearance. It quickly became clear that they didn't care. They waited for two days before going to Bill Smith's house. I found a yard truck in a sneaker that was unfamiliar to Smith, but didn't look any further.

They searched for Mitrice's car in jail and found personal items like her diary. Reading her last entry, they found that she was probably asleep for five nights.

Meanwhile, Lattice desperately called the Sheriffs to file a report of the missing person. Mitrice's missing case was transferred to the Los Angeles Police Department due to abundant resources, such as a search, but LAPD was actually an hour away from the Malibu/Lost Hills station where she disappeared. was.

(I don't know how much responsibility has been split between LAPD and LASD. The sheriff's department continued to be involved despite the transfer, and the investigation found it to be very irresponsible.)

The family was promised that a large two-day search would start Saturday, September 19, three days after Mitrice disappeared. They intended to pull all stops using helicopters, search dogs, and all the resources they had available.

But when the day came, there were four lawmakers who surveyed several neighborhoods in the area. At this point Mitrice was missing for three days and the police had virtually no information. I wasn't looking seriously. The search for the 19th ended before it got dark. It was intended to reopen on the 20th, but it never did. It was a full joke and a slap in the face to Mitrice's family, who became more and more convinced that police were simply not interested in finding her, according to all the explanations.

Unable to rely on the authorities, the family took the problem into their own hands. They spent the day making flyers, distributing them and conducting their own research.

Sheriff goes to defense
Meanwhile, after learning how terrible Mitrice's disappearance was, the sheriff began strict adherence to their actions on the night of her disappearance. They issued a statement aimed at justifying her arrest in the restaurant, but when she released her, she claimed to be perfectly fine:

"She was clear and showed no mental problems," said Steve Whitmore, a spokeswoman for the LA County Sheriff. Then he mentioned the drinking test she took at the restaurant.

But Lattice did not believe the word. The police were first called because the restaurant manager believed that Mitrice had a problem. Multiple people will back this up. Latex later said: "If the police officer saw her behavior and decided to conduct an open-drink test, he must have noticed something was wrong."

An excuse that the Sheriff has come up with to evolve Mitrice over time. They first claimed the prison was full (which later proved to be untrue). They said there was no reason to keep her there (even if they told Lattice not to release her until morning). Finally, the guards used the excuse that they weren't "babysitter service."

Sheriff Liebaka

Somewhat weird-Sheriff Baka was a Los Angeles County Sheriff from 1998 to 2014. A quick Google search for his name reveals that he is exactly the definition of "bad cop". He was involved in multiple scandals during his time as a sheriff, including lying to the FBI about the inmates' abuse in LA County Jail. In February 2020, he was sentenced to three years' imprisonment in La Tuna, a federal correctional facility in a lesser prison on the outskirts of El Paso, Texas, for obstructing the investigation.

Paul Tanaka, the second LASD commander, was sentenced to five years in prison for obstructing the same investigation. Tanaka also had a relationship with the white supreme gangster, Lynnwood Vikings (they sound like real stand-up guys, right?).

Baka was never interested in the Mitricese case and wanted to have nothing to do with her family. He has always avoided their demand for more information, for example security footage and his surrogates following his lead. Despite her family lying and gassing, he claimed that his department did nothing wrong.

Michael Richardson gets up

Michael Richardson decided it was enough, as he was dissatisfied with the lack of investigation into his daughter's disappearance. Why didn't Mitrice's lawsuit get noticed? Michael called Malibu Mayor Andy Stern and asked for more. Not particularly interested in Michael's story, Stern said he was on the way to a meeting and had no time to speak.

But Michael never intended to give up so easily. Stern was also a property owner in Malibu, with millions of dollars in fortune. Michael called him at the phone number of a real estate agency and told him this time he was a well-known soccer player interested in buying one of Stern's properties. This caught the attention of Stern. He canceled the planned meeting and offered to see him soon.

He was regretted when Stern learned who Michael was. Such a story would be really bad for him as the mayor. In November 2009, as a result of

Michael's efforts, the city of Malibu approved a reward of $15,000 for those who had information about the disappearance and current whereabouts of Mitricelli Richardson.

Finally, a real search

On January 10, the Sheriff's Office of Los Angeles finally carried out the type of search the Mitrice family wanted. One of LASD's most extensive searches of missing people to date. The search included 336 trained searchers who, with the help of dogs, dug up 18 square miles of ridges, canyons and trails on horseback. A helicopter picked up the explorer and dispatched it to an area difficult to reach.

The investigation did not reveal any evidence of the whereabouts of Mitrice, but Michael Richardson hoped his daughter was still missing.

"The beauty of today is that they couldn't find a corpse," he would have said after the search.

"Lost" video footage is displayed

Mitrice's family continued to request security footage from Lost Hills Station on the night she disappeared, but the request was ignored. They had been lying for a few months about whether it existed. It was until March 2010 that they were asked by the station to watch the night's footage (which seemed magical from the chief's desk drawer).

There were multiple red flags brought out by footage: one, the parts were edited. Soon Lattice was able to find out that her daughter wasn't well and not behaving like herself. She worried and acted in a manic manner. Footage of Mitrice in her cell showed that she was struggling and behaving erratically. "She is holding the door swinging back and forth," Latice said. "She is pulling behind her hair."

To Latice, it became much clearer that her daughter really suffered that night, and the agent showed no compassion or humanity for her. The information from LASD was sketchy and incomplete, so the true behavior of the night was not fully revealed.

Finally, as a result of being able to watch the footage, Lattice filed lawsuits against Los Angeles County and Sheriff officials for negligence and illegal death. She said the main reason for the lawsuit was to give them the right to request information about the night Richardson was arrested. Dismiss all police and criminals involved. "

Finally found Mitrice

On August 9, 2010, about 11 months after Mitrice went missing, it was discovered that everyone was afraid. Michael continued to hold hope for Mitrice somewhere, but Lattice began to accept the tragic reality that his daughter was almost certainly dead.

Around 1:00 pm, Park Rangers were patroling the rough canyons of the Dark Canyon in search of illegal marijuana cultivation operations known to occur at these locations for remote areas. Getting to these places is not easy. With no trails, you'll need to scale a steep rock face and cut through much of the wild undergrowth.

The area they were looking for was about 8 miles from the Sheriff's Station in Lost Hills and 2 miles from Bill Smith's house where Mitlis was last seen living. When they encountered a human skull, they were heading through a deep canyon. The park ranger called for discovery at 1:30 pm. The surrogate arrived around 3:00 pm and had to wait for the helicopter to land in the valley.

A team of seven arrived from the coroner's office at 5 pm. With the hope that they would have to follow standard protocols when the body was found, they photographed the body, inspected the site for clues, and established a crime scene. But this was not the case. At this point, we are not shocked to find out that the Sheriff's Office has completely interfered with the handling of Mitrice's remains. The detective was airlifted to the location of the body, but not the coroner's team. In fact, I don't think a coroner's team was ever airlifted. It's usually a complete departure from how crime scenes are handled.

Mitrice's family was informed that the body had been found and probably belonged to Mitrice. However, when the family asked them if they could come to the scene, the phone representative accused me of coming and meaning rudely. Latice asked how to treat the site, a crime scene, and when to remove her daughter's body. The deputy prime minister told Latice that the area would be secured and treated as a crime scene, and the rest would be airlifted in the morning because the night was too dark to take them there.

However, instead of doing what they say, at 8 pm that day, lawmakers randomly collected the artifacts they found and returned them to the station in a helicopter. Not surprisingly, they didn't look so difficult and were found to lack a lot of bone. The prosecutor's office was shocked by the actions of the sheriff department. As reported by the LA Times, the coroner claimed he was "very clear" with the sheriff officials [on how the remains should be dealt with], and police approved the coroner. I couldn't think of another case where I had moved the entire skeletal body without getting the money."

On 13 August, the sheriff sheriff issued a statement, announcing that the body found in the canyon belonged to Mitricelli Richardson. "There are no signs of murder at this time. I don't think the body can tell the story," he said. Baka further said they found only "skulls and some bones," which was not true. In fact, most of the mummified remains have also been discovered.

Latex convinced the idiots and sent her and a small group of close friends to the scene. They installed a small monument while they were there. Looking around, they found one of Mitrice's finger bones. This further indicated the carelessness of the security department when the Security Office was first on the scene.

How did Mitrice end there?

Despite allegations of no cheating from LASD, there is a lot of speculation about what actually happened to Mitrice that night (in this case, how badly they handled everything It is natural that there is doubt about the conclusion of). One LAPD detective later tells Los Angeles Magazine, "It sounds like someone kidnapped her, killed her, and at some point left her body abandoned."

Her clothes were a little above the canyon from most archaeological sites, with no evidence of being removed by the animals, suggesting that she or someone else had removed them.

Some bones, such as the femur, were also found in the middle of the canyon. Mitrice's hyoid would have been broken if it had been strangled, but could not be healed.

Mitrice's family and friends are convinced that her death was not accidental. Ronda Hampton, who was an intern for Mitrice, said. They never put out the possibility of murder there. Mitrice couldn't have been able to hike the canyon. "

We believe that some of the bodies have become mummified and may have been buried elsewhere, excavated, and later dumped in a canyon.

An official coroner's report states that her cause of death is unknown. If they were able to follow the proper procedure, they could have made a firmer decision.

Aftermath of Mitrique's death

Latice and Michael filed an unjustified death suit against LASD, saying Mitrice should not have been released from prison that night as it showed clear signs of mental instability. They were awarded $900,000.

The Mitrice family has never failed to pursue justice. In February 2016, California Attorney General Kamala Harris agreed to begin an investigation into the death of Mitrice after receiving a heartfelt letter from Michael Richardson.

"Well, Harris, I look at you and I can see Mitrice Richardson too. A young, smart, smart, black and beautiful young woman who crushed her butt at school one day helped and made a difference. Who will be able to give birth."

However, after investigating the case for about a year, AG Harris' office sent a letter to Michael Richardson, who found no evidence of misconduct in LASD's handling of Mitrice's case, so they decided to end the investigation. I explained. Michael was very disappointed with the decision and accused AG Harris of his interest only in his daughter's case while running for the US

Senate (elected in November 2016). "Kamala Harris is a fake," he said. "We don't need someone to guide us."

Another glimmer of hope came when Mitrice's memorial service at the New Testament Church in Los Angeles on September 7, 2019, announced that the new LA County Sheriff, Alex Villanueva, wanted to evaluate the entire case from day one. was. A set of fresh eyes. However, a few weeks later, Sheriff Villanueva rereads the department's investigation, saying there is "no reason to re-examine cases already under investigation in Los Angeles County, the office of the Attorney General's office." Announced not. Internal review of the local prosecutor's office and the sheriff's office. "

This was another blow to the family. Villanueva, in particular, was very lazy and useless during the investigation of Mitriche's disappearance and death, as it decided on the basis of incident reports by the Sheriff.

He considered LASD changes made to avoid what happened to Mitrice that happened to others. Now, a phone representative tells Latice that Mitrice has disappeared, so you can submit an adult missing report immediately instead of waiting 24 hours. The agent will verify that people have cell phones or other personal items before they are released from prison. Most importantly, Villanueva said that those presenting mental health problems would be evaluated before they were released.

According to Villanueva, Mitrice's lawsuit has never been settled and the ministry continues to welcome new information.

My thoughts

As I mentioned at the beginning of this work, I strongly believe that the money provided to police should be redistributed. Mental health services, for example, are scarcely underfunded. With the Mental Health Hotline in place, Mitrice Richardson will still be alive today.

The Mitrice case also raises a number of questions about the Department of Security's actions-how can they receive so much money and still fail victims and their families so miserably? They were lazy and careless both while Mitrice was in detention and during the investigation of her disappearance. What exactly was paid?

Another question to tackle, why didn't they bother? Was Mitrice a black woman? Was she a lesbian? If she was a white woman, would her disappearance be treated differently? In my opinion this is very likely.

Their actions certainly played the role of her death, even if they did not kill her directly. She would have gone home with her mother if they were accountable, had some sympathy and detained her as they said. Mitrice Richardson didn't have to die. Agents who have shown such explicit neglect of her life should be held accountable.

15 THE CANNIBAL WIFE

Katherine Knight, the first woman in Australian history sentenced to imprisonment without parole. Be prepared because this lady is a special kind of terrible thing.

I first heard about this case when watching a make-up tutorial video. Does it seem strange? I will explain. I haven't really put on makeup since March when I started working at home. "Do it yourself!" Oh, sweet...but not. Do you know how much I spent on makeup? I'm not wasting that beautiful shit on the same pair of PJs I've been wearing for two days while sitting in front of the TV.

I've seen Bailey Sarrians filling the holes in my mind's color pop palette size, as some of me are certainly deprived of the joy of makeup. Now, I thought I was too old to really understand YouTube's personality, but apparently I just needed to find the right person. Having found Bailey and her Mystery Makeup Monday series, my life will never be the same. It's makeup and a true crime story. When I grow up, I want to be her. I love her.

What do i not like? Kill your husband and try to eat him.

This case is messed up – from the beginning of Katherine Knight's life to her imprisonment. Hell, more than that. The woman says she is regularly visited in jail by the ghost of her dead uncle. Yes.

Now, I'm not the type to blame for the silly nurturing as a reason why people cease to be desirable members of society-we can all make the right or wrong choice. But tough childhood certainly does not help the overall outcome. Sometimes it distorts the young mind or exacerbates already if-y DNA.

Katherine Knight was born in October 1955 in Barbara Lofan and Ken Knight. Prior to the birth of Katherine, Barbara was married to Jack Lofan.

They had four sons. Barbara began an affair with Ken Knight, a close friend and colleague of Jack.

In the small, conservative town of Aberdeen in the Hunter Valley of New South Wales, Barbara and Ken's relationship led to a serious pearl-holding Bible verdict scandal. Local repulsion basically had to move Barbara and Ken, leaving her four sons behind. The new couple settled in Molly.

Barbara and Ken have four more daughters. The youngest is a set of twin girls, Joy and Katherine.

In 1959, Barbara's estranged husband, Jack, died. The two sons, who still lived with Jack at the time of Jack's death, moved with Ken and Barbara.

In an eight-person house, Ken was very alcoholic and enjoyed being very physically violent against Barbara. He is claimed to rape Barbara up to 10 times a day. Now, there's no doubt that this guy can be called a serious sex addict, or whatever, while he's extremely drunk ten times a day. It's not easy.

Barbara is a illustrious example of the motherhood she was, then goes to her four daughters and tells them all about the intimate details of her "sex life" with her father. She will hate Ken, hate all men, and weep and complain about how they were the same. All men were like Ken.

Katherine denies that his father was one of the perpetrators, but claims that she was frequently sexually assaulted by a grown-up family (her half brother?). This continued until she was 11 years old. Psychiatrists accept Katherine's allegations of assault, but doubting some of the details, her family confirmed that a general idea of the event had occurred.

So, of the ritualistic behavior of the mother, who used her daughter as her personal human diary for the perverts Katherine experienced during the abuse she suffered and all the dreadful details of her life. In the meantime Katherine grows distrustful and hates men?

Katherine attended Muswell Brook High School and was described as a lonely and bully who loves to eat small children. She assaulted at least one boy with a weapon and injured her teacher. The teacher had to defend himself against Katherine.

When she was 15, Katherine dropped out of school without really learning how to read and write. Difficult to read and write, Katherine began her "dream job" at a local slaughterhouse where she could see and participate in animal slaughter. She quickly became waterless (don't joke, don't joke, don't joke). .. Katherine put his butcher knife set on his bed and advertised, "It's convenient whenever I need them." Quote. This was a habit of continuing in every house where she lived until she was imprisoned.

In 1973, Katherine met David Kellet when he started working in the Aberdeen slaughterhouse. He was an avid and drunkard who lost his job working for the railroad at Coffs Harbor after the train took a school bus and killed six children. His heavy drinking was due to an accident and was eventually fired.

While he is dating Katherine, he sometimes becomes a "partner" with her twin sister. I don't know if this was intentional, an agreed deal, or if I was always drunk and indistinguishable. But in any situation, it's terrible.

In 1974 Katherine and David got married. She arrived at the bike service and David was already drunk on the altar. Obviously, the marriage got off to a great start. Barbara gave David some mother advice to marry her daughter. According to David Kelett, she said:

"You look at this well, she kills you. If you stir her the wrong way or do the wrong thing, you'll mess up. She'll kill you. She'll screw Is loosening."

If someone told me about who I was getting married to, I wouldn't be there like Julia Roberts' movie.

Barbara must have been a terrible psyche as Katherine tried to strangle David on their wedding night.

The wedding night was a sign that the entire marriage was violent and toxic. One time, Katherine, who was pregnant with her first child, came home late from the darts tournament, so she burned all David's clothing and put it on his head in a frying pan. David fled for life and was treated for a broken skull.

Police wanted to prosecute Katherine, but she promised David that she would change and was sufficient to convince him to drop the charges against her and return home.

In May 1976, shortly after the birth of his first child, Melissa, David left Katherine for another woman, took him to his fucking fractured skull in Katherine's abuse, and then with her mother. Moved to Queensland. The next day, in a clear spiritual break, Katherine saw a stroller pushing her newborn daughter down Aberdeen's main street. She was throwing a pram to the left and right and then slammed her baby in the public square. She was placed in a facility and diagnosed with postpartum depression. Katherine took weeks to recover before being released.

Shortly after being released, Katherine took Melissa along with her on an active railroad track, marching into the town with an ax, threatening to kill people. A local man, known to the townspeople as an "old Ted," heard Melissa's baby's voice and was looking for a railroad track when she literally rescued her just a few minutes before passing the train. It was

Katherine was arrested and taken back to a psychiatric hospital. Did anyone sign in the next day? Hospital staff claimed she had "recovered."

Surprisingly, she was undoubtedly not recovered, and less than a week after her release, Katherine brought one of her precious butcher's knives back into town. She was able to find a woman with a car, tear her face, force her into Queensland, and find David.

The women were able to escape when they stopped at the gas station, but by the time police arrived on the scene, Katherine had apparently repaired David's car, so he was going to kill him and put him at the gas station hostage. I was accompanied by a young mechanic, allowing him to leave. She told police that her intention was to go to Queensland and kill David and his mother.

Okay... and I can't do anything in the next part...

When David was informed of Katherine's intentions, he and his mother returned to Aberdeen to "support" Katherine.

David, why do I have to break my mind like this?

I think she thought she was taken care of by David and his mother when she was released from her mental hospital for the third time in August 1976. I think it's hard to break the cycle of abuse and perhaps he thought he was doing the right thing by becoming Katherine's head. It's still immeasurable that he'd delighted her back in consideration of everything he did to her, but when your feet are trapped in someone's snare, the logic disappears from the window. ..

In March 1980, they had a second child, a daughter named Natasha.

And here's the fucking kicker-in 1984, Katherine left David. She. left. he. Later all. At least David is free.

Katherine rented an apartment near her job at a slaughterhouse, but after hurt her back, she quit her job and was given a public housing in Aberdeen. Obviously for the next few men who still fall into her "charm."

In 1986, Katherine met David Sanders. Within a few months he moved to her house with his daughters, but he had his apartment in Scone. Shortly after moving, Katherine's abuse retreated his ugly head. She threw Thunders out of the house on a regular basis, feeling jealous of his actions and attention to his daughters when he was not at home.

The cycle continued many times. Sanders returned to his old apartment and Katherine appeared and begged him to come back. Things peaked in May 1987.

According to John Chillingworth, the father of his son Eric, he visits Katherine who is still in prison. He is quoted as saying to The Daily Mail:

"She regularly meets with psychiatrists and over the years she has done many self-improvement jobs. She loves pottery and painting. She seems calm... she Goes there with everyone and they call her "grandma". "

Katherine can die in prison, even though she hopes to someday be free to walk and meet her grandson to become part of the life of four children.

Chillingworth said: No, I don't think so... but will society accept her after being liberated? I would say no "

No, no.

Well, pour your thoughts into this crazy story and friends! There were so many really shocking moments, and so terrible and weird, that I was at a loss for painful comments.

I feel that there may have been some mental health interventions throughout Katherine's life, especially with regard to David Kellet, which would have saved John Price's life in the future. I know David and his mother tried it, but I understand that without the right resources, it was too much for them.

Unfortunately, David Price's life ended in one of the most gruesome ways I've ever read. And now his children, friends and family need to continue living without him. It has never been successful in intervening in domestic violence or mental health problems.

Domestic violence and abuse relationships can be fatal to this. There is always the possibility of someone losing their life. And unfortunately, it's a very poisonous endless cycle, as family and friends decide not to bow down for their mental health or really know why you got so far away .. I have been by myself. I will not spare the decision to leave someone in my life, but outsiders will be able to recognize small signs of abuse, listen to my intestines, raise my voice, ask questions, secure It is important not to be afraid to provide a place. Even if you are rejected. Especially in the current COVID era. Abuse rates are skyrocketing.

If you have an abusive relationship, please contact someone. Take that first step. I know it's scary, but it's worth it. It is better to be alone than to be lonely with others. It is intended to feel love, especially when someone else does not love you. Your friends and family want you to be safe, happy and free. You are not a burden.

16 THE ICE BOX MURDERS

This is the story of Fred and Edwina Rogers, literally dressed in ice.

Fred and Edwina Rogers (81 and 72 respectively) did not answer the phone for three days, and nephew Marvin Merlin was more and more concerned. Marvin decided to go to their house, but all the houses were confined and the blinds drawn were closed. He had no way to check his aunt and uncle, so he called the police and requested a welfare check.

Around 9 pm, two policemen took Marvin to Rogers' house and knocked on the door. When there was no answer, they kicked the door. There were no signs of an older couple or their 43-year-old son, Charles.

The 1.5-storey house was chaotic, but it didn't seem strange to him because Marvin said his aunt and uncle weren't the best housekeepers. What seemed weird was the moldy dinner at the table and the rotten smell coming from the 3x5 electric refrigerator in the kitchen.

When one police officer opened the refrigerator, he first saw what he thought to be washed but unwrapped "pork meat" lining all the shelves in the refrigerator. When he opened the sharper drawer, he found his first assumption very wrong.

The Amarillo Grove Times article describes the scene as follows: There was little food in the ice box. "

The crispy vegetables had a cut head of Fred and Edwina.

Following the murder investigation, Charles became the number one suspect. That is, who else wants to lock up their house after killing their parents in a very personal, demented way?

Investigators determined that Edwina was assaulted and subsequently fired in an executive style. Fred was hit with a claw hammer and died. His eyes were scooped from his skull and his genitals were removed.

According to Amarillo Grove Times quoted by Captain (then) LD Morrison, they were dragged into a bathtub downstairs after Fred and Edwina died. Here, the body was completely drained from the blood and the limbs and torso were cut into refrigerator-sized pieces. The couple's organs were later found in a nearby sewer-the murderer chopped them up and flushed them down the toilet.

The medical inspector is quoted by the Amarillo Grove Times as: Dismantling was a fairly decent job. If you're a murderer, I think it's good.

The blood and evidence of the house were carefully removed, but tests have shown that large amounts of blood have been removed from the bathroom floor and bath tub. The wooden staircase leading to Charles' bedroom was rubbed cleanly. In his room there was a large collection of clothes, hot plates, kettles, tableware and ham radio. There was also a bloody keyhole saw.

Authorities decided that they were looking for someone with anatomy experience. They believed that the keyhole saw was used to dismantle Fred and Edwina.

It was estimated that the Rogers family died for three days. That is, they were killed on Father's Day.

Charles Frederick Rogers, 43, is said to be very intelligent and have a strong interest in ham radio. He speaks seven languages and has a BS in Nuclear Physics. He was a US Navy pilot during World War II and served in the Navy Intelligence Service.

After discharge, he became a seismologist at Shell Oil Company. At some point in the 1950s, Charles was said to have been involved in a civil aviation patrol who met David Ferry.

You'd think it's crazy information that has nothing to do with the death of his parents, but just wait. It's going to be a little weird here.

After nine years with Shell, Charles confusedly quit his job without explanation and moved in with his parents, but they rarely saw his son. Charles turned lonely and a recluse, living in an attic bedroom and communicating only with his parents through a notebook passing under the bedroom door.

After the murder of Fred and Edwina, an international search for Charles began. Most of Roberts' neighbors were shocked to find out they had a son. Those who knew about Charles, like cousin Marvin, rarely left home, but when he did it, it was before dawn and did not return until it got dark.

It is completely unknown what he did throughout the day.

Despite a nationwide search, Charles would never be seen again.

Among them, the author-who was an investigator at the National Intelligence Service Bureau-claims that Charles was a CIA agent until the mid-1980s. They accuse Charles of being one of the guys who assassinated President John F. Kennedy and impersonating Lee Harvey Oswald in Mexico City.

Charles, along with Charles Harrelson (father of actor Woody Harrelson) and Sean Seeholt, who were arrested at Deeley Plaza after the assassination of Kennedy, were one of the "three wanderers," they say.

The author also claims that this is why Charles had to kill his parents-Edwina was listening and tracking Charles's CIA phone (I went through his landline phone at home) I think). be killed. Obviously, shredding them was the logical result.

According to the overgrown Noor man, Charles fled to Guatemala, where he probably died in old age.

This book has been severely criticized for its complete lack of sources of information and for its explicit and fictitious account of certain events, conversations, and thoughts of attribution. Go figure

The book admits that Charles was dealing with a CIA contract worker when he was a seismologist in Shell, but they need to dismiss their parents after hearing that Charles isn't secret. It completely rejects the idea that it was the CIA agent himself/Kennedy from the attic/secret phone about the killing. That is a strange sentence.

Instead, Gardenia believes that Charles was emotionally and physically abused by his father as a child and as an adult. Disconnecting his father's genitals on Father's Day, you know, it may confirm it a little.

They also found that near the end of their lives, Edwina and Fred both scammed their son, forged his signature on the transfer of land he owned, took a loan in his name, and made money. Claims to have been in his pocket. Gardenia calls Fred and Edwina the "scammers." They say Fred works as a bookmaker, regularly engages in gambling and fraud, steals large amounts of money from Charles, and continues to physically abuse the grown man.

Again, I think it's a chop chop.

Gardenia argued that Charles had planned his parents' deaths for years and would flee to Mexico using his "strong friends" whom he met through his ham radio hobbies while working in the oil industry. .. They finally showed that Charles theoretically ended up in Honduras and that he experienced some cosmic karma when he was killed in a wage dispute with a miner.

The Ice Box murder case is called "fact-based work of fiction."

Charles Rogers was legally sentenced to death in July 1975 by a judge in Houston.

The killing of Fred and Edwina Rogers remains an open case. Charles is still considered the only suspect.

The murdered house on 1815 Doris Call Street remained empty until it was demolished in 1972. By the year 2000 when the condominium was built, the lot was empty.

Ah, the circle of life.

This story goes through so many strange changes. When I first started reading it, I was shocked enough by the idea of the recluse son passing the notes under the door and chopping his parents and putting them in the fridge.

But the more research I did, the crazy it became.

To be honest, who has the time to fuck? But if you do, the Internet is a black hole that gets lost.

What do you think about this incident?

17 THE NUN KILLER

On the morning of October 31, 1981, in Amarillo, Texas, Sister Angela Martinez went to check Sisterta de Avents. Sister Angela was worried that Sister Tadea missed the morning chapel. It was totally different from her. Unlike me when I was growing up, Sister Tadea really wanted to go to worship.

On Sunday I had more false sore throats than I could shake the cross.

It was also completely different than the sisters Tadea closing the bedroom door. Sister Angela testified in court. "Sister Tadea was deaf and always kept the door open to hear the buzz in the morning. I knew it wasn't Tadea's fault, but I couldn't think of it further. Was too much. It was a shock."

Sister Angela was shocked when she opened her door when she found the nude of a 76-year-old nun with her arms out of the floor.

Sister Angela called on other nuns. They wrapped Sister Tadea's body in a sheet and cleaned the floor of blood stains. The supposed Tadea sisters died after they fell to the ground.

Later that day, another nun, Sister Florentine, found a broken window in the monastery's community room and noticed that there was an intrusion.

The nuns called the police to investigate and began discussing with the police whether they should talk about Sister Tadea. Sister Florantine told court during the trial: But I took it for granted that she died naturally, as others did. "

They hesitated to reveal a dead nun wrapped in a sheet in the next room, but police acted upon hearing the tweet.

In Sister's room, police collected knives from bed linen under the bed. Fingerprints from a broken window with a knife blade, bed headboard, and screen cut out. An additional knife was found outside the driveway.

Later, the bodies of Tadea sisters were autopsied. Examination revealed stings, head bruise, and neck abrasions. Signs of external bleeding and trauma indicated that the nun was raped. Hand strangulation was the rule of death.

Early in the investigation, police told witnesses who claimed to have seen 17-year-old Johnny Frank Garrett running from the direction of the monastery. Garrett lived opposite St. Francis.

Well, during my investigation, this witness didn't actually see Garrett leaving the scene, but he could have been a self-proclaimed seer named "Bubble" who had that "vision." You have to say what you have found. She portrayed a teenage boy wearing a "Afro-style wig" during an attack, running from this vision scene and standing about 5-11. Foam said the murderer lived on the same street as the monastery.

Police interrogated Garrett, searched his house, and found a knife that matched the one found in the monastery's driveway. His monastery also had his fingerprints, but it was where he regularly visited. Garrett's print was not a real murder weapon, but a knife under the bed.

Police announced the confession to Garrett as his own words, but he refused to sign the confession and swore he had never done so.

On November 9, Garrett, who was identified as a person with developmental disabilities in some reports, was arrested and charged with the murder of Sisterta de Avents.

In the trial, the prosecution presented their case in which Johnny Frank Garrett was looking for a nun who would take a knife from his home, cross the street early in Halloween, and invade the monastery to rape and kill him. After he was over, he ran back home, and that's when the witnesses saw him.

Garrett and his family maintained his innocence, but he was convicted and sentenced to death. He was taken to the Ellis Unit and detained as a death row prisoner.

His first execution date was set on January 6, 1992, but after intense pressure from the Union of Texas Bishops on the death penalty, Pope John II calls on Governor Texas Henry Richards for generosity. did.

Richards approved the request and accepted the stay. The Texas Pardon and Parole Commission held a hearing to discuss Garrett's transfer to prison life as requested by the Catholic authorities in Texas.

17 votes that the death penalty was not supported.

On February 11, 1992, Johnny Frank Garrett was executed by lethal injection in the Huntsville unit. He was 28 years old.

His last food request was ice cream. Official records state that Garrett refused to issue the final statement, but the last words were recorded by journalists at the time of execution, and they were quoted and regularly attributed to Garrett. ..

As reported by APBnews, Johnny Frank Garrett's last words were: "I would like to thank my family for loving and caring for me. I am innocent, so the rest of the world You can kiss his beloved ass."

And honestly, it feels great.

DNA evidence in the killing of the Tadea sisters was tested and linked to Leoncio Perez Rueda, especially considering over a decade later.

Police openly described the case as "too similar" to the killing of sisters Tadea, but the two cases are not related. However, the case was not resolved until a few years after Garrett was executed.

In 2004, DNA from the case of Sister Tadea was executed via CODIS. It is back as a match against the Cuban immigrant Leoncio Perez Rueda, a career criminal. He was one of the "criminals and unwanted" exiled to the United States by Castro during Mariel's boatlift.

And how did Rueda's DNA fit into the CODIS system? It was removed from the sheet under Nanny Bryson at the time of her killing.

Rueda was then sentenced to 45 years in prison for the murder of Bryson, which he confessed. When asked by the police about the DNA's agreement on the murder of Sister Tada'a, Rueda confessed in the past that he "murdered and raped a nun," but did not promise to be the murderer of Sister Tadea.

To date, Rueda has never been charged with the murder of Sister Tadea, and Texas has not admitted to murdering an innocent man.

There is no denying that some people are wasting oxygen on this planet, but until the standards of death penalty evidence are very high, an innocent person cannot squeak and corrupt a truly wicked person. can not.

There is a documentary on Garrett's case "The Last Word". Also a semi-fiction horror movie called the last word of Johnny Frank Garrett.

.

18 THE BEAR BROOK MURDERS

On November 10, 1985, Hunter was passing through Bearbrook State Park in Allenstown, Hampshire when he came across a 55 gallon metal drum. In the barrel, the hunter found a body of an adult woman and a young girl wrapped in plastic, perhaps in a trash bag.

Autopsy later determined that both victims had been killed by a traumatic blunt weapon. The body was partially deboned.

During the investigation, police also sought hints and information from across the United States and parts of Canada. The body was not identified despite hundreds of leads.

Scientific tests told investigators a few things about the victim. It was concluded that adult women are white with Native American ancestry. She was estimated to be between the ages of 23 and 33. Her hair was curly or wavy brown and was between 5'2" and 5'7" high. Her teeth revealed important dental work, including filling and extraction performed by specialists.

A young girl found in a drum with a woman was thought to be between the ages of 5 and 11. She had symptoms of pneumonia and crooked, bent front teeth. She had earrings on her ears, two earrings on each leaf, and was between 4'3" and 4'6" tall. Her hair was light brown with waves.

Fifteen years later, the incident was completely cold. Reconstruction of victims has been open for a long time, with no new leads or hints.

The body of the barrel remained unidentified.

Then in May 2000, a second drum was discovered not far from its original discovery in 1985. Inside this barrel were the bodies of two girls. Their bodies were completely skeletonized.

Autopsy revealed that both children were killed by a blunt trauma, just as the other two bodies were found a decade and a half ago. Police united all four victims and became known as the Arens Town Four.

The first of the two children died between the ages of two and four. She had a gap between her front teeth like the first young girl discovered in 1985. Her hair was brown and she was 3'8 inches tall. The girl had a bite, was probably noticeable when she was seen, and may have suffered from anemia.

The last child was estimated to be between the ages of 1 and 3 at the time of her death. She had blonde or light brown hair and was between 2'1" and 2'6" tall. She also had a gap between her front teeth.

All four victims are believed to have been killed between 1977 and 1981.

Once again, investigators begged the public for tips and leads, but none were solid, and Allenstown Four remained unknown.

In June 2013, investigators released an updated version of the victim's facial reconstruction created by the National Center for Missing and Exploited Children. This reconstruction has shown how their teeth can affect the appearance of their face.

Again, there are no leads.

In November 2015, the National Center for Missing and Exploited Children released the latest reconstruction photos of four victims at a press conference by the New Hampshire Attorney General's Office.

Rasmussen was born in Denver, Colorado in 1943, but grew up in Arizona. In April 1961, he joined the US Army (or Navy, depending on sources) and was discharged seven years later.

From 1967 to 1968, Rasmussen lived in Hawaii and met his first wife (the name is unknown and I can't blame her). In 1969, he and his new wife moved to Phoenix and began working as electricians as they grew up. family. Rasmussen moved to Redwood City, California around 1974. Just a short time later, his wife left Rasmussen and brought back four children. The last time Rasmussen's children saw their father was Christmas 1974.

In 1978, Rasmussen dated a woman named Marlyse Elizabeth Honeychurch. She finally lived in La Puente, California on Thanksgiving Day in 1978. During the vacation, Honey Church had family discussions with Rasmussen and his two daughters, 6-year-old Mary Elizabeth Vaughan and 1-year-old Sarah Lynn McWaters.

Rasmussen moved many times after his wife left him. And in 1979 he went to New Hampshire where he worked as an electrician under the name of Robert "Bob" T. Evans. During this time, a woman named Elizabeth Evans has been listed as a wife, but she has not been identified. I think it was Honey Church.

Rasmussen was arrested three times in 1980. Once to write a bad check, and second and third to steal electricity.

On November 26, 1981, 23-year-old Dennis Baudin attended a family Thanksgiving dinner for her six-month-old daughter and boyfriend Bob Evans (Goffstown, NH). This is the last time her family meets Dennis again. Sadly, she was never reported missing. At that time her family believed that she had left the town for financial reasons.

And what is this guy and Thanksgiving kidnapping?

Rasmussen stayed in New Hampshire and continued to own Bodin's baby daughter.

In March 1984, Rasmussen moved to Los Alamitos, Calif., under the name Curtis Mayo Kimball (MAYO?!). In May 1985, he was arrested at DUI in Cypress, California and booked under the alias Kimball.

By the beginning of 1986, Rasmussen had changed his name again. This time it's Gordon Jenson. Something more boring. He works for RV Park in Scotts Valley, California. After six months at RV Park, Rasmussen took off, but left "Little Lisa" with his neighbor. Police begin an investigation into Rasmussen, eventually matching Curtis Mayo Kimball's fingerprint with Gordon Jenson's fingerprint, and a warrant is issued for arrest.

It took more than two years before Rasmussen was arrested and was eventually handed over to a car stolen from Idaho in November 1988 to San

Luis Obispo, California. Rasmussen, among other things, has been charged with possession and abandonment of stolen vehicles. He is sentenced to three years in prison but is released on parole one year later. He withdrew immediately the next day.

Little is known about Rasmussen's life when Unsoon Jun, his unofficial wife from that time until June 2002, went missing. He was going by the name of Lawrence "Larry" William Bangna, and sometimes Dr. Bangna. He's daydreaming now

Jun was a Korean immigrant and biotechnology worker with a master's degree in chemistry from San Francisco State University. Jun hired a "handyman" in Rasmussen in 2000 and immediately began living with him and her boyfriend. The two had an informal wedding in the summer of 2001. This was the Star Trek theme.

It didn't take long before Jun complained that his friend Larry was lazy and wasn't interested in working or starting a family. In May 2002 she was missing.

Bangna gave multiple explanations for Jun's absence. The most popular excuse was that she went to Virginia or Oregon to work in the cabin. Within two months, Vanner made a purchase using Jun's credit card, and Jun's friends formally filed the missing person's report.

Investigators interviewed Vanner about his missing wife, who claimed she was fine, lived in Oregon, and worked in a hut. As you know, it's just plain, believable. However, the detective became aware that Bangna was talking about Jun in the past tense and was convinced that something bad had fallen on the chemist.

On September 26, 2002, police secured a warrant for the search for Jun and Ban's house. In the basement, they found a lot of cat litter piles on the floor, cats, axes, butchers and other tools near the litter that looked like hair and blood.

Upon closer inspection, the woman's mummified paw was still wearing sandals and protruding from under the kitten's toilet. Delving into the trash, police quickly find the rest of Jun's mummified remains.

Rasmussen was charged with murder and dismemberment. He did not object, but was eventually convicted and sentenced to 15 years in prison.

Fingerprints taken from "Vanner" reveal to police that their killer was using many other aliases. We tested the DNA to see if "Little Lisa" was biologically related to Rasmussen. It wasn't her.

In 2010, Rasmussen died of natural causes while in prison. He was 67 years old.

In 2015, with the help of a genetic ancestry, an adult "Little Lisa", now known as Dawn, found her mother's identity to be Baudun, and "Bana" was kidnapped, then Bob Evans, and then I learned a story called Curtis Mayo Kimball. .. This linked Vanner / Evans / Mayo to the area and time frame of the Bear Brook murder. Authorities immediately announced that Evans was suspected of killing Bear Brook.

The National Missing and Exploitable Children's Center found on 26 January 2017 that'Robert Evans' was the father of one of the children from the Bearbrook murder, but its name was false. I do not know the legal identity of a man. Police released a video of an interview with "Evans" (known at the time as Vanner).

Two months later, Vanner/Evans/Mayo was confirmed to be Terence Rasmussen, with evidence of DNA believed to have been provided by one of his sons born from their first marriage.

The method used to identify Rasmussen was used to identify Joseph James de Angelo in 2018 in the Golden State Killer case.

In June this year, investigators identified the victims of three other DNA-confirmed Bearbrook murders as Marlyse Elizabeth Honeychurch (b. 1954) and two daughters, Marie Elizabeth Vaughan (b. 1971).) And Sarah Lynn McWaters (b. 1977) – A former girlfriend in Rasmussen and her children who left with him in November 1978 after a family discussion over Thanksgiving.

The fourth child, found by the Honey Church family under the nickname "Angel" in a barrel, was confirmed via DNA to be Rasmussen's daughter, but Honey Church wasn't the mother, but the angel's. Whoever the mother was, she led the researchers to be perhaps another victim of Rasmussen. I don't know when Rasmussen met Angel's mother, but I think it was probably born between 1975 and 1976 in California, Texas, or Arizona.

It is unclear how long Angel was taking care of Rasmussen, but the investigators said in November 1981.

I believe he was killed with Honey Church and his daughters before leaving New Hampshire.

Today, police are trying to reveal the angel's real name and the identity of her mother. They are also looking for tips and leads on the whereabouts of Denise Bordan's body.

Rasmussen is the suspect for many other crimes.

In 1980, 14-year-old Lauren Lahn disappeared from Manchester, New Hampshire. Rasmussen lived a mile away from her.

Six weeks later, 23-year-old Dennis Denault is missing from a bar in Manchester. She lived on the same street as Rasmussen.

A woman was found in a refrigerator in an ice bag on March 29, 1995, in Holt, California. Her identity is still unknown. The time of her death is estimated to be sometime in 1994. The cause of death was determined to be blunt trauma. Jane Doe is estimated to have been between the ages of 24-45 at the time of her death and has strawberry blonde or red hair. She wore blue sweatshirts, Levi shorts and Gorilla brand hiking boots and weighed 110 to 130 pounds and was 5'5'.

If you have information about Jane Doe, please contact the San Joaquin County Sheriff's Office at 209-468-4572.

On August 23, 1975, a victim known only as turquoise du was found in Tilden Regional Park, Contra Costa County, California. She was killed four days before she was spotted with blunt trauma. She is believed to be between 18 and 30 years old with brown eyes and brown hair. She stood at 5'3" and 166 lbs. She wore a turquoise T-shirt and a thin chain with four turquoise stones and a matching ring.

If you have information about Turquoise Doe, please contact the Contra

Costa County Sheriff's Office (925-335-1500).

Of course, if you have information about Denise Beaudin, please contact Manchester Police at 603-668-8711 or 603-792-5505.

Terry Rasmussen had two victim types. He hunted for women and for children, but he liked them as a set. He will make friends with his mother who has children and will start dating her. He wanted to manipulate the woman to disappear spontaneously or to talk to her family.

Police say Rasmussen killed at least six victims.

This case trips me up. It was terrifying that these vulnerable women thought they had found a man who loved themselves and their children.

19 THE NINE MILLION DOLLAR MURDER

Cynthia Hoffman's family, 19 years old, had a daughter living with an intellectual disability, which enabled her to work at the second grade level.

"Her disability made her want friends," her father, Timothy Hoffman, told The Washington Post. "That's all she wanted, she just made her friends." It also made her vulnerable to being misled, manipulated and victimized.

On Sunday, June 2, Cynthia was going to see her father collecting the money that she borrowed from her recent handyman job that helped her. Timothy Hoffman thought something was wrong when she didn't show up. Cynthia was a good boy. She never ignored her family. She never answers the phone. She would never have gone home.

The next morning, when Cynthia had not yet appeared, her family officially reported to police that she was missing. The missing girl was last seen at a polar bear playground in Jack Springs Park, Russia, on Sunday afternoon, according to information from a friend of Cynthia who named himself Angela. She wore a hoodie, jeans and tennis shoes.

Angela was texting Timothy Hoffman while police were searching. Angela said to Timothy, "I hope she can come home safely. She is my best friend."

Angela's real name is Denali Bremer.

At the age of 18, he recently started an online friendship with a man named "Tyler" from Kansas. Tyler said he was a millionaire. After a while, Tyler confessed to Denali that she wanted to buy child pornography, and he needed her help to do that.

Denali sent Tyler an explicit photo of himself, but he wanted a younger one.

He provided her money to send her a photo of a young girl, and Denali responded accordingly with explicit pictures of a 15-year-old girl (name was withheld) and another 8 or 9 year old girl. Was sent to him. Denali used these young girls to take porn pictures and videos on her phone and texted Tyler.

But Tyler was still not happy. He wanted to raise his ante.

"I will rape and kill someone in Alaska," he asked. He told Denali to send him a video and a photo of the act. And if Denali did this, he promised to pay her $9 million.

Denali accepted the offer and recruited four friends to stop the crime.

On June 2, Denali and one of her conspirators, 16-year-old Cayden McIntosh (who was released because he was tried as an adult) rented a truck from his friend Calebrey Land to give Cynthia I picked it up.

They told Cynthia that they wanted to go on a hike, and she was happy to go along, completely unaware that in her truck her "friends" were all that was needed to kill her. It was

The three drove to the Thunderbird Falls Trail. A popular area for hiking through a mile of birch woods before reaching the 200-foot waterfall. When Denali and McIntosh found an isolated settlement, they abandoned the sidewalk and took another path along the Ekultna River.

Denali and McIntosh settled in a quiet, empty place, ambushed Cynthia, tied their hands and feet with duct tape, and wrapped them around their heads to completely cover their mouths. Denali then manufactured a 9mm handgun and aimed it at Cynthia, but she was unable to trigger it, according to the case's prosecution documents.

"Bremer tells [the detective]...she gave the gun to [McIntosh] and told him to shoot her because she couldn't do it, and he shot her."

Cynthia was shot behind his head.

They reportedly left her body on the river or near a trail/riverbank.

The day after the killing, police were searching near a polar bear playground based on a lead from "Angela" sent to Cynthia's father Timothy.

Police tried to contact a friend because she needed to know who she might have been with when Cynthia went missing. One friend, Denali Brehmer, consistently appeared in photos on Cynthia's Instagram account. In one image, Cynthia captioned the photo with a selfie of two girls. "

Police contacted Denali's mother and told her she needed to talk to her daughter. Was she in the park with Cynthia? Did she know what happened? Denali's mother told police she said her daughter thought she had been shot dead and pushed into the water. She didn't have any other details or places.

Denali was brought in for questioning. Like Cayden McIntosh, he was thought to have been in polar bear park that day.

During interrogation, police quickly learned that three teenagers were not near the polar bear park. This story and the text of "Angela" was a plan from the outset to drive the police and Cynthia's family and see them in the wrong place.

But this first-round question made the whole situation one big accident.

According to the indictment document, Denali and Macintosh shared a similar story when first asked.

The trio decided to drive around, smoke weeds, go to Thunderbird Falls and take a disturbing picture. They intended to tape each other like a hostage and take ducts in the order in which they took pictures for fun. As you know, that of a normal child. Denali told police that "she began to panic" when the tape was put on Cynthia's mouth.

Denali took the tape out of Cynthia's mouth to calm her down, but she began to react more and called the police, saying that her two friends had kidnapped her and raped her. I threatened to tell you. According to Denali, Mackintosh began to panic with the sounds of these threats, so he took the gun that Denali had (brought it only as a prop in the photo) and held Cynthia behind his head before Denali stopped him. Shot at.

The logistics of this first and first story are missing to me. Cynthia panicked her back, so she took the tape out of her mouth, but did you manage to shoot her behind her head and put the tape back in?

Yes.

Denali then claimed that Macintosh thought that Cynthia was trying to call the police because of her cramping, so he pushed her into the stream.

According to Macintosh's credit, he mainly backed this version of the event, saying that in fact all the trios agreed with the picture of the duct tape, but after Cynthia's panicked, he "blacked out." Insists. He vaguely remembers pulling the trigger and pushing his body into the river. He told police he wasn't sure if Cynthia was dead after shooting her, or if she was drowned.

Macintosh told the detective he didn't want Denali to go.

According to court documents, after leaving the scene, Macintosh burned Cynthia's wallet, clothes, her identity card, and the gun used to shoot her.

At this point, Macintosh was arrested on multiple charges, including first-degree murder and tampering with evidence. Somehow, Denali has been let go. The investigation continued.

While being held at the Anchorage Correctional Facility on Wednesday June 5, McIntosh told the other prisoners, all the shots were Denali's ideas, and the story he told police was bullshit and he didn't want to Denali. It is said that you have started to say that it is bad.

The next day, the detective of the case was presented with Denali's Snapchat story during an interview with her friend, who was not involved in the murder. In an online story, Denali says: If you get in touch with me I'll get in touch, but I won't come back for a long time...I will not come back for a long time. I'm sorry, I didn't mean to do that.

The detectives brought Denali into the second interview. This time, they learned about "Tyler" and his multi-million dollar offer. Denali acknowledged that the trip to Thunderbird Falls was planned by her and four friends, including truck owners Macintosh and Calebrayland. She told investigators that after Cynthia was detained, she gave a gun to Macintosh and was instructed to shoot Cynthia because she was not ordered to shoot Cynthia.

19-year-old Caleb Brayland has been admitted to Cynthia's involvement in the murder program and has been charged with conspiracy to commit the first murder and murder.

While planning to kidnap and murder Cynthia Hoffman, he admitted that there were two other men in the room, identified as boy men and boy women only. Both were charged as minors and taken to the McLaughlin Youth Center.

During interrogation, it was revealed that Leyland had sexually assaulted a boy's woman, which resulted in Leyland imposing an additional charge on him.

Police secured a search warrant for her phone and computer after Denali's admission, and actively searched for "Tyler." Only after the police returned to the police with evidence of Tyler's true identity, prosecutors learned that Denali was caught fishing for catfish.

"Tyler" is really 21-year-old Darin Schilmiller. He's from Indiana, not Kansas, and doesn't look like the photo I used in the conversation with Denali. And he is far from becoming a millionaire, even with the most liberal stretch of imagination. He's basically a broken ass dick hole who likes to mess up sexual shit and find a fooled girl to give it to him.

On Denali's phone, police found child pornography "obviously". Sill Miller is identified as "Babe" in Denali's contact list. Through text messages, she and Sill Miller detail plans to sexually assault a teenage girl and shoot for him.

"First go to buy weeds," Denali wrote to him. "She won't fight me because I want to make her taller for her."

According to court documents, he tells her in a text from Sillmiller: I don't deserve you either..."

Cece was Cynthia's nickname.

The FBI was involved in the incident when child pornography crossed state boundaries. Denali confessed that Sill Miller had instructed her to sexually assault two minors (15 and 8 or 9) and sent videos and photos.

The FBI was able to recover the 15-year-old video and photos that Denali sent to Sillmiller, but found no evidence of an attack on a young minor.

Investigators also failed to find evidence that Cynthia Hoffman was raped, as requested by Sill Miller.

Tyler: Let her tie her up if you have too

Bremer: Okay

Tyler: do a video

Bremer: OK

An excerpt of a text message between Denali Brehmer and Darin "Tyler" Schilmiller.
On Friday, Denali and Schiller were charged with the first murder charge, two second murder cases, and a solicitation for the first murder charges.

Shirumira was further charged with federal child pornography and is currently awaiting delivery to Alaska. It is not yet clear if Denali will face child pornography charges or sexual assault charges.

If convicted, an adult prosecuted may face up to 99 years in prison.

Through it, the community gathered around the Hoffmans.

Fundraising for a concert to fund the expense was held at the Carousel Lounge in Spenard. During Cynthia's funeral, a motorcycle procession moved with the family to the Cremation Society of Alaska.

Over 150 close friends, family and community members attended.

Cynthia's family says she most remembers her spirit and will miss it.

What do you think of your friends? This story is very crazy to me, but the top of the list is of those fucking shit that I believe Richie Rich in Kansas legally intends to pay millions of dollars to an amateur snuff. It is the stupidity and total falsehood of teens.

So he didn't even secretly demand it. You are not using the dark web. Just use your mobile phone and Facebook.

Even if you're not familiar with that kind of thing, at least you should be suspicious. It was obviously bullshit.

And now the completely sweet, innocent and loved young girl is dead. And five young people are losing their future.

20 BOBBY JOE LONG

Bobby Joe Long was born in October 1953 as Robert Joseph Long. His parents, Joe and Luella, grew up mostly with their mother because they broke up when he was a boy. The two were dysfunctional, to say the least. She worked at the bar, dressed in "Lacy" clothes, and brought back the revolving door of a man Long was upset and jealous of. Worse, he and his mother slept together until they were about 13 years old. And I don't know what it is unless it's a recipe to mess up sexual problems.

Long never had the easiest childhood. He failed in first grade, suffered multiple head injuries, and was mercilessly teased when he was adolescently attacked. The extra X chromosome caused him to develop breasts and the children were very cruel. He was later operated on to remove 6 pounds of extra tissue from his chest, but the emotional trauma remained.

In 1974, Long married a childhood lover Cynthia at the age of 22. They met at the age of 13 and spurred Long to start sleeping in his mother's bed. So, if anyone can do it, it's your tween girlfriend, right?

At their wedding, Long was in the Army stationed at Homestead Air Force Base in Florida. Cynthia and Long had two children, but I can't find any information. Probably the best. Things seemed to be going well for the young family until they hit the car while Long was riding his bike. He suffered a head injury and lost most of his legs. He was hospitalized for several weeks.

Cynthia says it was after this accident that Bobby Joe seemed to turn into another person (but I don't think we can put out all of Mama's sleep). Not only for his wife, but for their children. And his libido reached a whole new level, sometimes dangerous. Long believes that what made him hypersexual was traumatic mind from an accident.

Now that he is unemployed and out of the army, Long's sexual desires are all consumed. After being released from the hospital, he came up with a MO that would give him the opportunity to rape an unsuspecting housewife.

Between 1980 and 1983, Long became known as the "Classifieds Rape." It's not catchy, but who is complaining? He is responsible for raping at least 50 women in Fort Lauderdale, Ocala, Miami and Dade counties.

Long responded to a job advertisement on small appliances and furniture paper and scouted a "sale" sign for his home. If the person he met was found to be a woman living alone, or if her husband was not there for the day, he made a knife, tied him up and raped him. Before leaving, he robbed them. Just add salt into the wound for fun.

Cynthia never doubted what Long was doing now, but she found out that their marriage had collapsed. She applied for a divorce.

For the single, Long moved in with his friend Sharon Richards. Although it doesn't take long for their roommates, Richards accused him of raping Long. Long was released because police did not have enough evidence to accuse him. A few weeks later, furious with Richards, Long beat him in the middle of the debate and retreated.

In July 1983, Long began dating a 17-year-old girl who worked as a nurse in a local hospital. He regularly gave jewelry to his new girlfriend. Unknown to her, the jewelry was stolen from his rape victim.

A few months later, Sharon Richards returned to Long's life, pursuing alleged assault on him in the 1981 incident that hit him. Long was found guilty at the trial, angry, writing dozens of letters to the presiding judge, and vowed that he had not committed all the charges, so he begged for a trial. In the real case of "what happens only to white men in the judicial system," Long's request for retrial was granted by a judge. The second time, all charges were dismissed. When Long left the court, Long laughed with Richards' face.

In November 1983, Long was charged with sending obscene letters and sexual pictures to a 12-year-old girl in Tampa. Police also had a record of the phone calls that Long made to the child. This gave him a 2-day sentence and a 6-month probation. Perhaps the last two days have really taught him lessons.

In the early 1980s, Hillsboro County averaged 30 to 35 murders a year. County murder statistics suddenly escalated while Long was under probation in 1984. Someone kidnapped, detained, raped, killed a woman and threw her body in unusual positions and poses about once every two weeks.

On March 27, 1984, Nuunti Long, also known as Lana Long, was missing for three days when discovered by a group of boys in a remote area in southern Hillsboro County late in the afternoon. She is a 20-year-old exotic dancer who had problems with drug addiction.

Lana lay with her back down with her hands tied behind her with rope and cloth. The same rope was found around the neck in a "chain-like" extension. There was a potential cloth gag around her face, and her legs were more than 5 feet apart, so police speculated that she was intentionally displayed this way.

Police collected a variety of fibers from the body, including tire impressions, hair samples, and red nylon.

Lana Long's discovery launched an eight-month thorough investigation to find a serial killer working at a pace police never saw.

Two weeks later, the body of a young Caucasian woman was found in an isolated area of Hillsboro County. She was naked and her clothes were nearby. The victim was on her back, her hands tied to her waist, and tied around her neck. Her throat was cut and she had a blunt trauma to her head. She was later identified as 22-year-old Michelle Dennis Sims, a known sex worker in the area.

The ligature around the Sims neck was made of the same type of rope as Lana Long, and the tire impressions found in the scene were in line with those of the long scene tires. The detective officially linked both cases.

On June 24, Elizabeth Rudenbach was found in an orange grove. She was completely dressed and her body was in the process of breaking down, making her difficult to identify. Her total body weight, including her clothes, was only 25 pounds. Like the previous two victims, the ligature was not found, and because she wasn't placed anywhere near Interstate, investigators believed her murder was related. did not. They polygraphed Ludenbach's boyfriend and made something he failed to him a very good suspect in her murder. However, the forensic results have since returned. The red carpet fibers in Ludenbach's clothing were the same as those in Lana and The Sims.

Ludenbach was 22 and worked on the assembly line. Although she didn't seem to have a history of drug use or prostitution, she is known to frequent the Nebraska Avenue area, usually with Sims and Lana in the same location.

On October 7, the nudity of a young black woman lying next to a dirt entry road on a cattle farm was discovered. With the exception of the brassiere, all the victim's clothing was next to the body. The bra was tied in a knot and was hanging from the entrance gate.

Autopsy revealed a sting on the back of the neck, but a bullet on the head was the official cause of death.

The victim was identified as Chanel Devon Williams, an 18-year-old sex worker commonly found in the Nebraska Avenue area.

At this point, there were four known casualties, so police requested the FBI for a profile of the murderer.

On the morning of October 14, the body of a nude Caucasian woman was found below her waist in an orange orchard about 30 feet from a dirt road in northeast Hillsboro County. The corpse was placed on a gold bedspread. The victim's hand was tied in front with a red and white handkerchief. Her right wrist and leg were tied with a white string. The victim's leg was tied with a drawstring and the ligature was clearly visible in the victim's throat. She was hit on the head and strangled.

The victim was Karen Beth Dinsfriend, 28 years old. She was known as a cocaine user and sex worker who worked regularly in the Nebraska Avenue area.

During a forensic investigation, a red nylon fiber was found in Dinsfriend's body that matched all other crime scenes. They also found brown pubic hair on the bedspread with semen.

Two weeks later, a mummified corpse of a white woman was discovered near a highway in northern Hillsboro County. No clothing, ligatures, or other physical evidence was found on site due to the length of time the body was exposed to the elements.

The body was later identified as Kimberly Kyle Hopps, 22, after the arrest of Bobby Joe Long. He called Hops "sugar." Comparing the hair on her head with the hair found on Long's car, she officially became one of Long's victims.

A 17-year-old Lisa McVey quit her job at a donut shop on November 3 after being taken away from her bicycle by Long, who fell from the back of a parked car and fell. McBay was struck by a gun and brought back to Long's apartment.

McBay said in an interview with Fox. "He detained me with a gun for 26 hours. He raped me many times. I lost a number."

Using his past experience of street smart and sexual abuse, McVey tried to get in touch with her abductor. "I said," Listen, I'm sorry we met, but I can be your girlfriend. I can take care of you and no one needs to know. ""

"I talked to him like I was four," she says. And it worked. "

Recalling what he saw on the detective show, McBay said he wanted to have every piece of information he could collect for the police to help them catch the abductee if they survived. for. From under the blindfold, McBay stripped away everything he saw, from Long's car's "Magnum" nameplate to the number of steps leading to the apartment. And when she was in the bathroom alone, she purposely fingerprinted every surface possible.

"He laid his hands on his face at once," said McBay by trying to see the captor without actually seeing him, by touching his features. "It had pockmarks, a small mustache, small ears, short hair, a clean cut, a kind of ruggedness, but not overweight. A big man."

After spending time together, McBay began telling Long that he had a sick father that only he could do. She could play him having some sympathy for her, so she continued to play that angle. Eventually, Long loaded McBay into the car and drove her to a place on Hillsborough Avenue, not too far from where she abducted her.

He told her to wait 5 minutes before she could remove the blindfold, then he drove away.

"I put on my blindfold. The first thing I saw was this a beautiful oak tree. It's the moment I find out that my life is about to change for good. I saw a branch of a new life. "

On November 6, a female body was discovered just north of the Hillsboro County Line in Pasco County. All that remained was scattered bones and ligatures. Another ligature was found on the arm bone. Shirts, underwear, and some jewelry were also found near the bone, along with the hair of a person presumed to have come from the victim.

The Hillsboro murderer, who heard about the bones, met with a Pasco County detective and associated the bones with other victims based on ligatures left on the scene. During forensic investigation of evidence, there was little evidence for exposure and degradation, but a red fiber was eventually found that was consistent with all other suspected victims of the serial killer.

The victim was identified as 18-year-old Virginia Johnson from Connecticut. She worked as a sex worker between her hometown and the North Tampa area. She was officially a victim of Long, as she did in Hop, by the movement of her hair in Long's car.

On November 13, police spent the greatest break in the case, as a forensic analysis of McVey's clothing found the same red fiber as all the victims of the murder case. The police witnessed for the first time. And she was armed with a great deal of information about her kidnappers.

During an extensive interview, McBay told police that she suspected Long had stopped at a 24-hour ATM to withdraw money around 3:00 am. She explained that the vehicle she was on was a red car with a red interior and carpet, and the word "Magnum" was on the dashboard.

Investigators quickly jumped into this information and acquired DMV records for all Dodge Magnum 1978s, the only car with a "Magnum" on the dashboard, and roughly at the time McBay remembered stopping. Received a subpoena for all ATM cameras.

On November 24, the nude of a young woman was found on a hill on a remote road. All around me was a jeans patch and a top with blue flowers. The victim was found wearing knee-high stockings, head down, face down. There were ligature marks on the front of the neck of the body and on both the wrists and arms, but no ligature was found. Red fibers were found during a forensic investigation.

The victim has been identified as Kim Marie Swan, a 21-year-old female drug user who worked as an exotic dancer. She was last seen on November 11th.

The police finally have access to all the ATM photos and have begun to compare them with DMV records. This eventually revealed the name of Robert Joseph Long.

Task Force members began searching areas where the victim was often known and looked for Long's car. One team member noticed that Red Dodge Magnum was driving on Nebraska Avenue, and stopped the car in the guise that police were looking for robbery suspects. Cops asked Long if he could take a picture of himself so the victim could exclude him. I agreed for a long time.

The photo was returned to McBay, who clearly identified Long as her captor. Both arrest warrants and search warrants have been created and approved.

Long was arrested two hours later.

His car was searched and killed by investigators while he was being interviewed.

Long initially denied any knowledge or involvement in the murder, but confessed when McBay was raised. He briefly explained each murder. In each case, Long spoke to the victim in the car and immediately took control of the victim with a knife or gun to take them to various locations where they could be detained, raped and killed.

Long then drew a map showing where he placed the victims, including two unknown to the police.

The Hillsborough County Attorney and Public Security Attorney's Office has conducted a judicial deal on eight Lisa McBay murders and abductions and rapes. On September 24, 1985, Long condemned all crimes, 26 life imprisonment without parole, seven life imprisonment with possible parole 25 years later, and death sentence for the murder of Michel Dennis Sims. received.

On April 23, 2019, after serving 35 years in prison, Florida governor Ron De Santis finally signed Long's death warrant. Long will run on May 23rd.

Lisa McBay attends the execution. She is currently acting as a Sheriff for the Hillsborough County Sheriff's Office. She has one daughter.

21 BRADFORD BISHOP, FUGITIVE

Bradford Bishop was born in 1936. He graduated from Yale in 1959 with a bachelor's degree in history and a bachelor's degree in American studies based on several reports. He then earned a master's degree in international studies and a master's degree in Italian from Middlebury University. He also holds a master's degree in African studies from UCLA.

After graduating from Yale, Bishop married his high school lover Annette Weiss. Together they had three sons – William III, Brenton and Jeffrey.

After Yale, as a career, Bishop pursued a service life and joined the US military. He spent four years in anti-intelligence activities. He learned to speak fluent French, Serbo-Croatian and Spanish in addition to the already spoken English and Italian.

After finishing his time with the Army, Bishop joined the US Department of State to work for overseas services and made many posts abroad at places like Verona, Milan, and Florence. In Florence, he pursued a scholar again and undertook a postgraduate job at the University of Florence. I never know what this intelligent thing looks like. It's kind of trivial.

In 1972 he left Italy to work in posts in African countries including Ethiopia and Botswana.

In 1974, Bishop was assigned a new position. This time I'm in Washington DC. The family left Botswana and returned to America. Annette, her three sons, and her mother, Lobelia, settled in Bethesda, Maryland.

In early 1976, Bishop was denied promotion. The bishop was typical of what he was known to have, despite the fact that most of them had been denied promotion and their colleagues were provided by senior management explaining that their funds did not leave room for a raise. Took less "deny" than the strength.

Colleagues slowly took over his bad mood and complained about the failure to promote, as well as the constant fight between his wife Annette and her 68-year-old mother, Lobelia. . He said both women bothered him for being "washed out" and "stepping on the water" in his work, in other words not going anywhere.

On the other hand, how brave are they? But, on the other hand, it's not really a reason to kill anyone.

A colleague would later have known the bishop and his attitude towards his "enemy" and would have said, "I want to put them in their place."

The working theory of the causes that led to the tragic event of March 1, 1976, was a combination of the disappointment of the promotion and all the perceived ones issued by women of his life at home. It's about pushing the edges.

There are multiple motivations. Bishops reportedly had financial problems, but there were disagreements about severity. The Washington Post reported in 1986 that the problem was "mild" and "familiar with most upward mobile families." John E. Douglas described them as "nothing terribly unusual for people in their thirties living in such neighborhoods." In 2013, Bethesda Magazine reported that the IRS was auditing the family for financial problems, but it has not been confirmed.

At the time of the murder, Bishop lived with depression and insomnia. He was taking Cerax (oxazepam) to help with treatment.

On the day of the murder, Bishop told his secretary that he was uncomfortable and needed to see his doctor. (That means how disappointing you can be as a professional if you have a secretary, but I'm aside...)

Instead of going to the clinic, Bishop returned home, but he first stopped at four places along the way.

His first visit was in his bank, where he withdrew hundreds of dollars.

Next, he went to Montgomery Mall. Here he bought a hammer and a gas can.

Third, there was a gas station across the mall. He stopped here to fill the cans and station wagons.

Fourth, he drove to Pok's hardware store and bought a shovel and a rake.

After the shopping was over, he headed home and the police believe he arrived between 7:30 and 8 PM. It is believed that he first killed Annette and beat her with a sledgehammer. She was found next to the book while she was reading it. Then 14-year-old William, 10-year-old Brenton, and 5-year-old Jeffrey were killed in their bed. Bishop finally killed her mother and caught her when she returned home from a walk with her family dog.

And I know what you think, but don't worry, the dog was fine.

After the family's death, Bishop loaded each of the bodies into a station wagon and traveled overnight to a dense forest about five miles outside of Columbia, North Carolina.

He arrived early on March 2nd. In the swamp, the bishop dug wide but shallow holes and piled up corpses. He threw them in cans of gasoline, set fire to his dead family and left the scene.

Forest guards in North Carolina noticed the heavy smoke swirling in the sky and set out to investigate. The horrific scene he discovered was reported to local police, and an investigation was underway immediately. Discovered with the body were a gas can, a rake, and a shovel that Bishop purchased from the pouch hardware. The label was still on, and police were able to trace it to the local Bethesda store. In addition, some of the victim's clothing was labeled with Bethesda's expensive department store.

North Carolina police contacted Bethesda police, but at the time there were no reports of missing persons matching the victims.

Six days later, the bishop's neighbor contacted the police on suspicion of a sudden absence. When police arrived home, they found blood at the front door. This was a reasonable reason to enter the house. Inside, police found more blood as they walked up the entrance, hallways and stairs. Blood spilled to the ceiling in the bedroom.

Police recalled an inquiry from North Carolina police a few days ago and kept in touch with them about the possible incident. The burned body found in the swamp was identified as a bishop family through dental records.

As the bishop's investigation went smoothly, witnesses witnessed buying a pair of tennis shoes on the same day the bishop burned his body at a sports equipment store in Jacksonville, Jacksonville, NC. saw. They said the bishop was carrying a family dog and was probably accompanied by a "dark skinned" woman.

When I searched the family home, I couldn't find the Bishop's Smith & Wesson M&P .358 Special, and Yale Klasling. He is also believed to have his diplomatic passport. All family passports were found at home, but he was not.

On March 18, a 1974 Chevy Station wagon in Elkmont, Tennessee's Great Smoky Mountain National Park was abandoned approximately 400 miles (640 km) from a burn in the Columbia area. Upon inspecting the car, police found a dog treat, a bloody blanket, a shotgun, an ax, a shaving kit containing Bishop's pills, and a receipt Bishop bought the day before. The well of the spare tire on the trunk was full of blood.

Hiker witnesses believed that the car was abandoned there around 5 March. Known as an avid outdoor man who was in good shape and loved camping and hiking, police theorized that Bishop joined the Appalachian Trail hiker stream and disappeared into the wilderness. They tried to pick up his scent with Bloodhound, but with no success.

On March 19, a grand jury charged the bishop with five first-time murders.

Bishop had about a week ago time before the police really started looking for him. With his diplomatic passport with him, his money, his pilot's license and his dependable intelligence training, it is widely accepted that Bishop fled the county without being discovered.

Since his disappearance, there have been several bishopping sightings in various European countries such as Italy, Belgium, the United Kingdom, Finland, Germany, Greece, Switzerland, the Netherlands and Sweden.

In July 1978, a Swedish woman who worked with Bishop when she was transferred to Ethiopia discovered the Bishop twice in Stockholm. She was convinced it was him, but didn't know he was a fugitive and didn't report to the police.

In January 1978, a former bishop of the US State Department used the bathroom in Sorrento, Italy. When he entered, he admitted that the bearded man was convinced that he was a bishop. An eyewitness said, "Hey, you're Brad Bishop, right?" The man panicked, leaving the toilet immediately after answering "Oh no" with a clear American accent. Outside witnesses saw the bearded man flee to the alley.

On September 19, 1994, in Basel, Switzerland, a former neighbor of the Bethesda Bishop reported that she was on vacation and she saw the Bishop on a train platform.

As of 2010, authorities believed the bishop lived in Switzerland or Italy, or perhaps California, where he might have been a teacher or involved in criminal activity.

In 2014, the body of an unidentified man resembling a bishop was unearthed by the FBI after being killed by a car while walking along the Alabama Highway in 1981. DNA tests have proved that the dead man is not a bishop.

On April 10, 2014, Bishop was added to the FBI's 10 Most Wanted Lists.

Later in the year, the FBI requested forensic artist Karen Taylor to create an age-progressing sculpture of Project Bishop's 77-year-old appearance.

The FBI is still actively pursuing all the tips it encounters with lawsuits, but in 2018, Bishop was removed from the Ten Most Wanted list to make room for other more familiar criminals.

22 THE SAN FRANCISCO WITCH KILLERS

It was 1977. Phoenix, Arizona.

James Carson was a master's degree responsible family who chose to be the father of the five-year-old daughter Jennifer's house. But something about his behavior was changing. James was always a little hippie, but his wife, Lynn, was worried about increased drug use and flare temper. Lynn decided that she could no longer stay in a toxic situation, so she took Jennifer away.

But when James met Susan Barnes at a party in 1978, his interest in making compensation with his family rapidly diminished.

Susan was the mother of two teenage boys. She and James fell in love immediately and deeply. James moved to Susan's house shortly after seeing him. They adopted a full hippie lifestyle and became very heavy on drugs, especially acids. James abandoned James Carson and took on the new name of becoming Michael Bear. He told the young girl in a letter that "God" personally gave this new name.

Jennifer, Michael's first-married daughter, said in a 2018 article in the Huffington Post: He had a new name, a new personality, a new life... he was no longer the attentive, at-home father I remembered. My father braided my hair and read a book. But Michael Bear barely looked at me. "

Jennifer said staying at Susan's house was basically a nightmare. She said she was beaten and starved during her visit with her father. She slept in a sleeping bag on the floor and noticed that she had very little furniture in her house except for the aquarium in the master bedroom. She climbed a counter in the kitchen trying to find food. Her first choice was to always try to wake up her father and his new girlfriend, but often they were fainted after dropping acid all night.

Jennifer eventually found the courage to tell his mother that he really liked visiting his father. When Lynn lifted the young girl's shirt and got angry and found her back blushing from Susan's claws, Lin promised Jennifer that she no longer needed to be with her father.

It was around this time that Michael and Susan decided to sell Susan's home and become a nomad all over Europe. They married, left the country and traveled to Isreal, India, France and England.

Lyn and Jennifer also left the town on this occasion. They first settled in Southern California with Lynn's uncle. He was once a policeman and believed in his frightened niece without hesitation. Ling traveled several times for fear of her safety, blocking all communication with each other's contacts that could reveal her whereabouts to Michael.

It settled in the Hate Ashbury district of San Francisco in 1980, when Michael and Susan returned to America after a two-year trip. The birthplace of hippie culture, it is called drug, art, mysticism, and general counterculture. Kuma-san felt like at home.

Susan believed he was a mystic with knowledge of past, present, and future events. And during the vision caused by LSD, she claimed that the appearance of the Prophet revealed a list of all witches in the world. She said the "god" wanted her and Michael to kill them all. It was a "holy war against witches."

The list included, among other things, President Ronald Reagan and Governor Jerry Brown.

Susan rattled from the list during her vision, and Michael wrote it down, including a detailed plan of how they would kill Reagan.

Bears declared a "vegetarian Islamic warrior" who believed "magic, homosexuality and abortion" were destroying the world, and it was up to them to stop it "for the country's future" was.

22-year-old Kellin Barnes (not related to Susan) is an ambitious Georgian actress who became a bear and roommate when she moved to San Francisco to pursue her acting dreams.

In March 1981, she was found dead in an apartment she shared with Susan and Michael. Kerin was stabbed 13 times and her skull was crushed. Her body was wrapped in a blanket and hidden in the basement of the building. The Bears fled the scene after the killings, and they were not found anywhere by the time police considered them the first suspects.

Susan believed he was "ordered" to kill Kerlin during a storm, and every time she thought of killing Kerin, she struck a thunder, like confirmation. The Bears believed that Kellin was the witch who stole Susan's "health and power of yoga."

By spring 1982, the Bears had evaded police and moved to Alderpoint, California. They find work and shelter on a marijuana farm, where they spend days convincing their colleagues that a nuclear apocalypse is imminent and that the Anarchist Revolution is the only one that can stop it. Will be.

That May, Michael disagreed with fellow farmer Clark Stevens. The battle ended when Michael shot Stevens' head twice.

The bear tried to dispose of the body by burning it in the woods and filling it under chicken manure. They fled the farm. When Stevens was reported missing two weeks later, Humboldt County Sheriff began a search for Stevens around the farm, seeing his body partially burned in the woods. discovered.

Police immediately considered Suspect Bears as they disappeared after the death of Clark Stevens. They left their belongings on the farm and police treated them as evidence. Among what they left was a rebel manifesto containing a list of celebrities and politicians they were going to assassinate.

After this manifesto was discovered by police, Jennifer said she and her mother first learned of her father's crimes. "In 1982, a secret service appeared at the door."

Police and secret services have had problems tracking Bears' whereabouts. They were anti-government and easily adapted to life outside the grid. An entire state investigation was underway. Michael was randomly arrested in a hitchhiking in Los Angeles in November 1982. However, due to police negligence, he was released immediately and disappeared again before the Humboldt County detective intervened.

The following January, Bears was hitchhiking near Bakersfield, California. It was when John Charles Helier, a 30-year-old man driving to Santa Rosa on the 101 highway, caught them.

While riding, Susan was overcome with the vision that Heliyar was a witch and needed to be killed. The Bears physically attacked him while Hellyar was driving. Hellyar stopped the car and tried to escape, but outside the car the fight was deadly. While Heliar and Michael struggled for a gun that Michael pulled, Susan pulled a knife and stabbed him.

Being stabbed, Heliel abandoned his hold on the gun and gave Michael the opportunity to shoot Helial-with a clear view of the driver, who was called by one of the police. Police approached the scene, followed by high-speed pursuits, and the Bears tried to escape in Helier's car. They didn't go far because the police were able to stop the car.

The bear was caught.

The Bears initially agreed to hold a press conference to confess the murder that was charged. But before this happened, they withdrew their confession and acquitted in trial.

On June 12, 1984, they were convicted of the killing of Kerrin Barnes and sentenced to 25 years in prison. In additional trials, they were subsequently convicted of the murder of Clark Stevens, where they were sentenced to fifty years. They were found guilty and sentenced to a further 75 years in the trial of the killing of John Hellier. Both have filed multiple appeals, but all beliefs have been upheld.

A five-hour interview with the San Francisco Chronicle, a murderer, and a local television station made the Bears clear about their motives and guilt. They claimed to be pacifists who converted to an Islamic form and shared a religious mission: exterminating all witches from society. The newspaper dubbed them a witch-kill in San Francisco.

They claimed to know that Kerrin Burns was a witch because she falsely converted their religion. The alleged Clark Stevens deserved to die because he sexually assaulted Susan. Heliel called Susan the "witch" and said she sexually attacked her. Mr. Susan said Mr. Helier was "devilish."

In 2015, both Michael and Susan were released on parole. Michael canceled his hearing and said his beliefs about why he committed these murders remained unchanged and refused to show remorse. To a prison official, he wrote: I do not abandon my beliefs and have not abandoned them, so no one intends to release me on parole. "

Similarly, Susan refused to show remorse, did not help her lawyer, and eventually did not attend the hearing. Later she was refused parole. Both will qualify again in 2030.

To date, neither Michael nor Susan has shown remorse for their actions.

It should be noted that Jennifer should be careful with the victim's family to protest both her father's and stepmother's parole. She says she will continue to do so whenever a hearing is held. She last met her father when she was 19 years old. She visited him in prison. In a 2006 interview, Jennifer said: "It was like looking into the eyes of a soulless person. [He] is pure evil."

The Bears are suspected of killing nearly a dozen other people in the United States and Europe they traveled to.

Michael is in prison in Mule Creek State Jail. Susan is in a women's facility in Central California.

23 CHRISTMAS EVE MASSACRE

This is The Covina Massacre.

Divorce has never been so easy. But it's especially difficult if the two shouldn't have been married, and if one of them happens to loosen the screw.

Silvia Ortega and Bruce Paldo were married in January 2006, but shortly after the wedding it became clear that there was no problem between them.

Of their problems, Pardo's refusal to help raise three new stepchildren of his wife caused the greatest friction between the couple. Pardo refused to open a joint account with his wife, believing that Sylvia should take care of her own children on her finances.

After marrying a child with someone, everyone will have different views on what a stepmother should or should not offer. As myself, as a family parent, I choose to be financially involved because it works best for my family.

But what matters here is what works most effectively. Not all families or marriages are the same. And the most important thing you do when you marry someone with a child or someone who is a stepmother to your child is to discuss that it all works out. What are your expectations? Where can I compromise? If you can't compromise, is it a trade breaker?

You will never get into a mixed family situation without first discussing these great life decisions or experiencing the kind of problems that Pardos faces very quickly.

One year after getting married, Pardos applied for divorce. In June 2008, the legal battles intensified and Bruce Pard was ordered to pay $10,000 as part of the divorce settlement and about $1800 a month to support his spouse. Sylvia was allowed to have a wedding ring and pet dog. In his filings, Pardo complained that his ex-wife lived with his parents without rent, generously spent money, and took a vacation on his dime.

After a while, Bruce confessed to a colleague that Sylvia was "taking him to a sweeper," and he was worried about how to pay for everything. Just one month after the conversation, Pardo was dismissed from his job as an electrician who charged an incorrect time to raise his paycheck.

On December 18, 2008, the divorce between Sylvia Ortega Pardo and Bruce Pardo was confirmed and the order to support Bruce's spouse was suspended due to financial difficulties.

At 11:30 pm on December 24, 2008, Bruce Pald appeared at his former home in law in Covina, California, a city in the suburbs of Los Angeles. Joseph and Alicia Ortega hosted a family Christmas party for about 25 people.

Pald, dressed in Santa's suit, knocked on the door with a gift-wrapped package. There was a homemade flamethrower inside. Meanwhile, he had a 9mm semi-automatic pistol. The other three 9mm pistols were hidden in Santa's suit.

The door was opened by Sylvia's eight-year-old daughter, Leticia. Pardo shot her face. When party members screamed and tried to escape, Pardo indiscriminately fired a bullet at a moving target in the house, but police apparently executed Pardo, standing on numerous victims. I believe you did.

After all the ammunition had been consumed, Pardo sprinkled racing fuel around the house. Next, I unpacked the package containing the flamethrower and used it to burn the entire scene.

Pard fled on a Dodge Caliber rental car as one survivor called the police after competing from home to neighborhood. Soon, I got another 911 call from my neighbor.

"Come in immediately! They are burning someone's house," exclaimed one caller. Other callers even reported the sound of shooting.

Fire and police were immediately dispatched to the house, but by the time they arrived they all seemed completely confused, and the flames crossed the house and neighbors into a panic on the street and exceeded 50 feet. .. "When I arrived, it would be accurate to describe it as apocalyptic," explained one scene.

Eighty firefighters took almost two hours to extinguish the house. By the time it was under control, the damage had been so severe that the victim had to be identified by dental records. Sylvia and her paralets were initially declared missing by authorities until the body was proven.

Almost immediately, police received a tip from a neighbor and saw a man disguised as Santa leave the scene around 11:45 pm-only 15 minutes after the first shot sounded. The neighbor was able to describe the car and provide the plate number. The APB was in Pardo's car, but it wasn't necessary – there was a police call in Sylmar, CA, about 30 miles from Ortega's house. Brad Pardo found his brother sitting in a car outside his home and went home.

During an investigation into Bruce Pardo's body, police discovered that a piece of his Santa's suit had melted into his skin while using a flamethrower. His arms and hands were covered with third degree burns.

Also, the car had $17,000 wrapped around Pardo's legs. The Dodge was also equipped to explode with black powder if the rest of Santa's suit was removed from the vehicle. Because of this, there are some questions as to whether Pardo was always intended to commit suicide.

Pardo had four pistols with a capacity of 13 rounds and at least 200 ammunition. Treating the car as a bomb threat, police launched an incendiary bomb on the vehicle and destroyed it. At Pardo's house, police recovered five empty boxes of semi-automatic pistol ammunition, two shotguns, and a container of high-octane fuel tank petrol.

Police described Pard's house as a "virtual bomb factory."

That day, 9 people died and 3 were injured. Eight-year-old Leticia left a gunshot on her face-her injury was described as severe, but not life-threatening. A 16-year-old girl was shot in the back but recovered, and a 20-year-old woman jumped through a window on the second floor and escaped from the house before her ankle fractured.

The nine dead victims ranged in age from a 17-year-old boy (Silvia's nephew Michael Ortiz who died in a fire) to Joseph, Silvia's 80-year-old father who died of multiple gunshot wounds. Sylvia's mother, her two brothers, her two sister-in-law and her sister all died from a combination of gunshot wounds and fire.

In total, 14 children lost either or both parents on Christmas Eve 2008.

It's a crazy Christmas story. Much more messed up than Scrooge who scared me shit when I was a kid. Even the muppet version.

But I want all of you to really incorporate the story of Sylvia Pardo. Life was lost during a happy family gathering.

Let's take a look at family and friends and holiday celebrations. I really appreciate everything I see, no matter how big or small.

You are alive And so are your people.

Give them a hug. Tell them that you love them.

24 20 YEARS MISSING & A CHRISTMAS SUICIDE

The story you're about to hear spans twenty years, starting with a toddler who went missing over Christmas in 1977.

Dearborn, Michigan. Jarrett Betterson was not with his parents-in-law, Bill and Mary Klingel. He always felt that their acceptance of them was artificial. He knew they wouldn't approve their white daughter, Susan, who is dating a black man.

What made things worse between Jarrett and Klingers was that on Labor Day 1977, driving Jarrett, the car in which Susan and her two-year-old daughter Nicole were on the road took control. It was when I lost it. The car took a few revolutions before it stopped. Susan was thrown out of the car during the accident and died on the scene.

Jarrett and Nicole were not injured.

Police found marijuana in the car and wanted to accuse Jarrett of the vehicle murder, but sloppy police work prevented the DA from claiming these charges.

A few months later, during Christmas, Jarrett and his new girlfriend, Barbara, told Klingel that they were moving west to start a new life. "I am a good mother for Nicole. Barbara promised Susan's parents just before leaving home.

Klingel hurt. First, their daughter was taken away from their lives, and now their granddaughter. They asked exactly where Jarrett and Barbara would go, but they didn't give a definite answer. I didn't have an address. Klingers didn't know when to see his granddaughter. All they left was a picture of a toddler with her dark curly hair and a sweet smile.

Twenty years later, in 1997, Klingers was aged and desperate to find the only place where his family ties remained. They thought Nicole was 22 years old, old enough to decide if he wanted a relationship with his grandparents.

They hired a local private detective, Peggy Bezy. Shortly thereafter, she found Jarrett and Barbara Betterson living in Las Vegas. They were poor, lived poorly, and far from the glitz and light of the city centre. However, in all the searches, Peggy found no trace of Nicole in any of the records retrieved. In fact, there was no evidence that Nicole arrived in Las Vegas.

It was as if the girl hadn't existed since 1978...except for the Social Security department.

Until Nicole's 18th birthday, she was sent a monthly allowance for her family. And each month, the check was received at the post office by Jarrett Betterson.

Peggy Veggie knew that he needed help in Vegas to continue the lawsuit, so he contacted a private detective named Jeff Rosgen. Especially in Las Vegas, Rosgen didn't particularly like the missing suit. The town was big, busy and transient. Missing people had difficulty cracking. But Nicole's incident made him interesting.

Bezy had already scrutinized the records of schools, adoptions and hospitals. Whatever she can get. Rosgen went one step further, investigating family courts, police records, and DMVs.

nothing. After she left Michigan, there were no traces of Nicole.

Intrigued and confused by the incident, Rosgen decided to approach Jarrett with a long shot. He will tell a lie. bluff. Tell him that you just know what happened to Nicole and you just need to hear it from Jarrett's mouth. And if he doesn't get angry, he'll be taken before the grand jury and spend the rest of his life in prison. But the promise of generosity would have been hanging. It's a gift if Jarrett just opens and tells him what happened to Nicole.

It was November 1977 when Loggen knocked on Jarrett's door.

"I know what happened to your daughter," Rosgen said. "The whole story will make it easier."

Jarrett was panicked and scared. Roggen could see it in his eyes. But Jarrett sat in his electric wheelchair and closed the door.

Four days later, Rosgen received a phone call from Jarrett. He told Rosgen he knew he had to work with him. His time is over, he had to get rid of it. But he needed time to sort out the problem. He asked for 10 days. Ten days later, he set up a meeting between Nicole and Rosgen, and all the story came out.

Ten days have passed and Jarrett calls Rosgen. He needs more time. 10 days was not enough. Rosgen reluctantly agreed, but repeatedly called Jarrett to ask what was taking so long. Eventually Jarrett stopped answering the phone and Rosgen had a Christmas holiday.

The day after Christmas, Rosgen returned to his office, back to the mass of messages and voicemail, and the deadly progress of the incident. He picked up the phone and called for the murder.

There were multiple eviction notices for unpaid rent at the front doors of Jarrett and Barbara apartments. It's been three weeks since the apartment manager received contact from either Betterson, so he joined the unit. He called the police when the smell hit him.

Las Vegas police treated the deaths of 49-year-old Jarrett Betterson and his wife, 50-year-old Barbara, as murder-suicide.

In the apartment, police found that electric wheelchair Jarrett was forced to use after a bus accident. In the bathroom, Barbara's vial showed that she suffered a serious medical problem.

When they entered the master bedroom, Barbara lay on her bed holding the Bible and the cross. Jarrett shot the heart twice with a .22 caliber rifle, then made a bed and placed a red rose on his chest.

After that, Jarrett entered the adjacent room, covered himself with a blanket, and shot a bullet at the brain.

There was no record of suicide. "Please forgive me that I have to deal with the confusion left by the manager."

Las Vegas police decided that this was a fairly compelling and dry case, and was trying to put it all to bed when Rosgen called. "This has a twist," he told police lieutenant Wayne Petersen.

Faced with prison or death, Bettersons seemed to choose death. But apparently, what Jarrett didn't know was that there was no lawsuit against him. There was no evidence of crime and no body. There was no chance that he would face prison time. Rothgen really had a mystery about the missing girl and the feeling that only Jarrett and Barbara were the two who could answer the question. What happened to Nicole?

Barbara was mailing a letter to Jarrett's mother during Rothgen's visit and his death. She was contacted by her son and daughter-in-law for the first time in 20 years when Joni Betterson found it in a mailbox.

The letter says: Jarrett is about to go to jail, and I don't want to live without him. I'm sorry to be separated from my family. I'm sorry a lot. We have had a sad and difficult life. We wanted our trouble not to touch the family, so we protected ourselves. We tried to obey God. It's time for him to judge us. Go to your Bible and see peace. Forgive all the wounds we have given to your heart with the tragic and youthful blunder. "

They enclosed a $900 money order and asked for it to be used for their cremation. They wanted to mix the ashes in the same urn.

If she is still alive, there is no mention of Nicole, who would have been 22 years old when her father died.

Police believe Nicole may live somewhere without knowing who she really is. Probably sold by drugs or distributed somewhere between Michigan and Las Vegas. If she grew up with another family, she probably wouldn't know she was the little girl her grandparents were looking for. I have no idea what the new name, new family, and where she came from.

But police are more likely, says Nicole is dead. Perhaps she was making a fuss in the car on the way to the west and tried to quiet her who became violent. Perhaps Jarrett and Barbara panicked and buried her body somewhere along the road, in a remote grave. Something that is unlikely ever.

Around 2017, the DNA profile of a Nichols family was read into a national database, by chance, one day it could match something in the system. Klingers then died and never got the answer to what happened to his granddaughter.

Nicole Betterson is 42 or 43 today.

Now who is depressed? That's a very sad story. It makes me feel.

In my opinion, the Bettersons accidentally killed Nicole while traveling west, leaving her body somewhere.

20 years. They click together to collect the benefits of Nikole's survivors, after which the detective appears, asks basic questions, and adds a little heat to them, they commit suicide.

It yells me Guilty. So is the memo sent to Jarrett's mother. Especially "youthful blunder" is a phrase that sticks out to me. Sounds like they're wrongly chalking the death of a child

Barbara seems to have spent 20 years telling her that Nicole's death was an acceptable event, because she was young and unfamiliar with herself.

Also, in not having a clear understanding of what happened to Nicole in the last letter, in all that Barbara told himself for many years, "It was a youthful blunder," It means she didn't really believe in herself. Therefore, we couldn't say "we killed her." Admitting she was a murder could not be called out loud, even in the face of death.

Guilty.

What do you think, guys? Do you have a theory? Do you think Nicole is still alive somewhere?

25 A GHASTLY HALLOWEEN DOUBLE MURDER

Roommates Adrian Insonya, Leslie Mazzara, and Lauren Meanza decide to call the Trick or Treater the night after they have given away the candies. It was 11 pm when three 26-year-old women who shared a house on Dorset Street, Napa Valley, California, went to bed.

Outside, a man looked at his house. He waited, smoked a cigarette, and dropped a cigarette butt in the garden. When the house was dark and quiet, the man crouched through the unlocked first floor kitchen window.

Loren, who had only one bedroom on the first floor, woke up to the sound coming from the second floor. She sneaked quietly and slowly from her room, trying to figure out what she was listening to. Then came the one she said, "bloody, horrifying screams," saying the glass would break. Suddenly, the footsteps down the stairs were thundering overhead.

Loren bolted from the house using the backyard and hid in the backyard. She was confined, and she remained hidden, fearing that the person at home would come for her next. She heard footsteps echoing in the night sky as she saw an intruder climb through the same window and escape.

Meanza returned home when she felt safe to do so. She headed to her friend's bedroom on the second floor and found Leslie Mazzara face down in her pool of blood at the door of the bedroom. Meanza finds Adrian alive, crouching behind Leslie's bed, but bleeding heavily from multiple stings. Loren tried to dial 911 using his desk phone, but was disconnected. She raced for her cell phone, ran away from home, and drove her in her car, fearing she might still be at risk.

When police and paramedics arrived on the scene, Leslie Mazara was officially declared dead, but Adriane Insonya was still alive. Paramedics began working to stabilize her, but Adrian died before they could take her to the hospital.

Both women were stabbed multiple times.

Meanza told the police what she had heard, but because she was hiding, she was too scared to see the man leaving the house and could not explain the murderer.

The horrifying murder shocked the inhabitants of the gateway to the country of wine. The two women were extroverted, kind, and liked by their neighbors.

There was no murder in this town for four years.

"The killing affected everyone," says one local. "It was as if a Halloween movie was realized."

Leslie Mazara, a former Beauty Queen (Miss Williamston) from South Carolina, moved to the Napa Valley just that year to get closer to her mother. She worked at a nearby Rutherford winery. She was described by her friends and family as having a cheerful personality that could raise the mood of everyone around her.

In the summer of 2004, Leslie rented a house on Dorset Street and moved in with Adriane Insogna and Lauren Meanza, who needed a third roommate to split their rent.

An enthusiastic volleyball player, Adriane was a stranger who never knew he would close his phone when he died. The accident left her short-term memory loss and reading difficulties. Nevertheless, her natural person eventually gave her a college scholarship. She became a civil engineer and, after graduating, got a job in the Napa Hygiene District.

She met Lily Prudhome in this job. The two women became best friends. Lilly spent the night with her fiancé Eric Cople in a shared house in Adriane.

After the killing, police and forensic investigators struggled to capture the scene for evidence. And over the next 11 months, they interviewed more than

1300 people and collected 218 DNA samples determined to resolve the crime.

On September 22, 2005, police issued a statement saying there was a match between evidence of blood DNA found on-site and cigarette butt found outdoors. In addition, tobacco brands are very rare – Camel Turkey Gold. By publishing this information, police hope to establish a connection and give names to people who smoked that particular brand.

A few days later, on September 27, police surprised Eric Copple, the husband of Adriane's friend Lily Prudhomme, embarked on the killing of Leslie Mazzara and Adriane Insonia.

Camel Turkish Gold was a brand of Cople. Fearing to be caught was a matter of time, Copple confessed to his family and his new wife. He was convinced that he needed to submit himself.

“Eric didn't look stressed or depressed,” says a family friend. "He was an ordinary man."

The motives for the killing have not been officially announced so far, and Cople himself was unable to justify or explain his actions and told police during the interview that he had little recollection of what had happened. It was But the theory most likely believed by the authorities is that Copple felt threatened by the close friendship between their fiances Lily and Adriane Insogna at the time. He was afraid that Lily spending time with Adriane might come in a relationship with his future wife.

Copple has never met Leslie Mazzara when he visited Adriane's house, and it is unknown why he killed her. Was her bedroom the first bedroom he entered and was confusing her with Adriane? Did he mean to kill all of the house, knowing that there were two girls living there, other than Adriane?

Adriane, who police believe, died when he went to the rescue of Mazara after hearing a friend's screams. Before he overwhelmed her, she scratched and beat Copple-which left him on the scene to match his blood to the cigarette butts.

Leslie Meanza has been plagued by survivor guilt since that night.

In court, the couple regretted his actions and said, "I'm a broken man. I can't understand the explanation for my sinful deeds... the terrible pain given to many. Words Avoid me."

Two weeks after the murder, Lily Prudhome prepared a candlelight for her friend. Then, in February 2005, Lily asked Arlene's mother, Arlene Allen, to read a passage from the Bible during the ceremony.

"I looked directly into both of their eyes and read, "Love is stronger than death, and passion is more like a grave," says Allen. "I know Lilly chose those poems in honor of Adrian."

Lily says on her part he did not know that the man she married was responsible for the killing of a friend. During the trial, Lilly told the court: I told him, "Eric, there is nothing you can do in this world to make me love you." These words apply to you today as much as you did this afternoon. "

Eric Copple was charged with murder for the second time, abandoning the trial and pleading guilty to both. After discussions with the victim's family, Copple's lawyer, and the prosecution, Copple agreed to spend the rest of his life in prison without the possibility of parole, instead of withdrawing the death penalty. He also waived his right of appeal and the right to speak of the case to anyone except members of the clergy. That is, media interviews are not allowed, and even if he ever understood what that motive was, we might not be able to hear his motive.

Leslie's mother, Kathy Harrington, told Cople at the hearing of the judgment: I wish I could tell you I forgive you. Not at this time. And finally, I pray that my mother's child will never grow into a murderer. "

After the trial, Adrian's mother said, "I'm happy with the result, which is the best thing that can happen to all the families involved," Allen said. "I don't want to spend the rest of my life worrying about what Kople is doing. I want to continue my life. I don't know if I call this closure, but the solution There is a workaround. I love my daughter so much and I miss her deeply. The door never closes. I suffered a huge loss that never disappeared."

26 BRUCE MCARTHUR, SERIAL KILLER

Thomas Donald Bruce MacArthur was born in Lindsey, Ontario in 1951 and grew up on a farm just outside Woodville. MacArthur's classmates remember that he wasn't a perfect fit, trying to become his teacher's pet and becoming the tutortail of his class.

Both his parents were pious, but because of their different beliefs, MacArthur always lived with his mother. The chooser caused a ridicule from his rigid father. MacArthur later wondered if his father could possibly feel that he was gay and deeply disapproved.

At that time, MacArthur's sexuality was considered extraordinary, especially to the devout, so it was very difficult to accept what he knew was true. Instead, he pretended to be a heterosexual and proceeded.

In high school, MacArthur dated Janice Campbell. Both of them graduated in 1970. MacArthur received a higher education in common business programs. When he and Campbell were 23, they got married and moved to Toronto.

After decriminalizing the behavior of adults of the same sex in 1969, a "gay village" began to form in Toronto between College Street and Wellesley Street. MacArthur worked a few blocks from the gay village.

In the early 80s, MacArthur and his wife had a daughter, Melanie, and a son, Todd. After settling in the Oshawa community, MacArthur began to get deeply involved in his local church to distract him from examining his homosexuality.

But by the early 90's, MacArthur could no longer deny his sexual drive, and he began to have relationships with men. A year later he came out to his wife, but they decided to live together while they were married. They continued to commit to their faith and the belief that they could overcome their desire to be with MacArthur men. Around 1993, MacArthur lost his job and he and his wife faced financial ruin due to the legal challenges of their son Todd.

Todd faced criminal lawsuits forcing an obscene call to a woman he didn't know and requiring his parents to spend thousands of dollars on legal costs. In 1997, MacArthur and his wife were forced to remortgage their homes. Stress, sexual problems, and legal problems were their victims, and MacArthur and his wife decided to part.

MacArthur was technically single and Oshawa did not have an engrossing gay community, so he decided to return to Toronto. It becomes a normal face. It was here that he met a man, who pursued a four-year relationship.

His divorce was also confirmed when MacArthur and his boyfriend parted. MacArthur began seeing a psychiatrist to help him cope with stress and was prescribed Prozac for several months. It was around this time that I started working as a self-employed landscape architect.

… Violence begins here.

What caused MacArthur to snap? The end of his relationship? His divorce? Or was this always in him?

On a Halloween afternoon in 2001, MacArthur was invited to a sex worker's apartment she met in a gay chat room. They had sex a few weeks ago. The man wanted to show MacArthur a Halloween outfit. MacArthur was carrying a pipe with him, and when he was walking to the apartment behind the man, he hit him on the head. After defeating the man, he escaped from the scene.

The victim became unconscious, but when he came, he was alone in the apartment and called in the ambulance.

He was treated for damage to his head and body, requiring some sutures on his scalp and his fingers and 6 weeks of physical therapy.

MacArthur later claimed to have made an attack, but didn't know why he did it, and told police he couldn't remember what he did.

MacArthur was found guilty of being attacked with weapons and causing physical harm. Originally believed by prosecutors to justify prison terms, psychological and pre-judgment reports had a low risk of MacArthur recidivizing, and there were no "absolutely visible" signs of psychosis. "

Regarding MacArthur's personality, psychiatric reports describe him as "characteristically passive and indecisive" and maintain the image of "being a proper and supportive person and tending to act correctly and calmly." Said he is trying. But it also states that his "overt cooperativity may hide strong rebellious feelings that may sometimes break through his relevance and restraint."

There was concern that MacArthur's attack was motivated by a combination of the drugs he was taking with the illegal drug "Poppers," which enhances sexual pleasure.

MacArthur spent the first year of his sentence under house arrest, followed by a curfew at 10:00 pm for six months, and then three years for probation. During this time, he was excluded from the gay village except for work and medical appointments. He had to be at least 10 meters away from the victim at all times and could not spend with the "male prostitute". He was not allowed to own a firearm, nor could he buy or consume drugs without a prescription. Specifically, he was to own Popper.

Since April 2008, MacArthur has filed his conviction and was granted his pardon. It was wiped clean from his records and did not appear in subsequent criminal background investigations.

Most records and exhibits were destroyed in 2010, subject to the retention policy of the Toronto Police Service. The only documents that survived were a transcript of the guilty plea and hearing of the judgment, psychiatric and pre-judgment reports ordered during the trial, and photographs of the victim's injury and weapons.

In 2002, MacArthur registered with Recon while his assault was still in court- Recon-A gay fetish dating app for men who are in BDSM and looking for partners with similar trends. is. According to his profile, he was looking for a "submissive" man.

He thrived on almost every gay dating app and site and was able to profile with Silverdaddies, Manjam, Grindr, Bear411, BearForest, Scruff and Daddyhunt under the "Silver Fox" handle.

He was already well known throughout the community when the expulsion from the gay village was withdrawn in 2003. He has built a reputation for BDSM, violent sex and explosive temper. Men seen with him were sometimes warned to stay away from MacArthur and spread disturbing stories about him.

MacArthur shouted after saying he was warned not to get involved with MacArthur, according to potential fellow Robert James. You are like the rest of them! You think I'm crazy! "

By 2011, MacArthur had joined Facebook to proudly display photos of parties, vacations, birthday dinners, and concerts. A young man of South Asian and Middle Eastern descent frequently appeared in his photographs. Following probation, he was able to return to the gay village and became a regular at the bar. He lived in an apartment on the 19th floor at Leaside Towers in Thorncliffe Park.

MacArthur was run under the name Artistic Designs and had a successful landscaping business. Most of his clients are elderly, wealthy women that MacArthur found attractive, and he has built a client base through personal recommendations. A former colleague who set up a water facility as part of MacArthur's project said that he was accompanied by an older Caucasian who appears to have always been romantically involved with MacArthur and a day laborer, usually of Southeast Asian or Middle Eastern descent. Said.

Over the years, his son Todd was reportedly having a hard time accepting his father's sexuality, and the relationship was tense. Moreover, he was still facing legal issues. In 2014, Todd was sentenced to 14 months in prison for calling again an obscene call to a woman. He was released on bail, under his father's supervision in a Macarthur apartment in Toronto, and ordered to help with the landscaping business.

Todd's friend visited overnight. When he went to the bathroom, a friend discovered that the bathroom wall was adorned with a picture of an erected naked man. Most men seemed to be "Eastern Indians," according to a friend, and Todd said he was all men his father knew. MacArthur didn't try to hide the fact and laughed about it the next day at breakfast.

Missing from the village

The Toronto Police launched a long 18-month investigation in November 2012 to investigate the disappearance of the Scandalaj "Scanda" Navaratnam. In response to their "online cannibalization ring" tip, they formed a task force called Project Houston, which was eventually discounted.

Meanwhile, MTF identified two other missing persons related to geography and lifestyle. Abdulbasir "Basir" Faizi and Majeed "Hamid" Kayhan. These men, along with Scanda, were middle-aged immigrants from South Asia who disappeared between 2010 and 2012.

Faithie and Kaihan were married to women and had a double life. Police associated them with a gay village, where they disappeared.

An anonymous chip directed police to McArthur, who was linked to two men missing via a dating app. He was interviewed in 2013 as a possible witness.

Project Houston served as a solid leader in the disappearance case – James Alex Brunton. He was 69 and had a lot in common with MacArthur. He was eventually identified as a suspect for the disappearance of three men, but possessed, created, distributed child pornography, and a "cannibalizing sexual contract" with a teen from Colorado. I pleaded guilty to the conclusion.

Shortly after, Project Houston had no evidence to identify the suspect.

The day after the 2017 Pride Parade in Toronto, 49-year-old Andrew Kinsman disappeared. He was last seen living near his residence. Two days later, after discovering that no one had seen Kinsman, his friend had access to his apartment. They reported no signs of turmoil, but found the Kinsman cat to be deficient in food and water. The next day, they reported the disappearance of Kinsman to police.

Unlike the other three missing men, Kinsman was openly gay and a proud member of the community with deep roots and friendship. He has long been a volunteer with the Toronto People's with the AIDS Foundation and was the administrator of his building. He was known to be stable and responsible, and friends did not believe he would leave without prescription medication. And surely he would have made some arrangements for the cat he loved.

Kinsman was active on social media, but police found his phone hung up on the day he disappeared. Kinsman was on the street for 6 feet 4 inches and 220 pounds, so he was almost never the victim of violence unless he knew the attacker.

..

Kinsman's disappearance has spurred the founding of an online group in the Toronto gay community dedicated to finding him – find Andrew Kinsman and the Missing Rainbow Community in Toronto. Their goal was to raise awareness with missing person posters and a survey of organized volunteers.

Shortly after these groups were created, pictures of 12 missing people from the gay community began to be distributed online. Upon receiving the information, five men were already found and one died of suicide. Unidentified men were three project Houston victims, Kinsman, and Selim Esen, who disappeared on April 14, 2017. The disappearance was related.

We have a clear understanding of who MacArthur is, what he is doing, and how his family situation has been for decades. And we know that men are missing, and the gay community wants some answers.

It's 2017 and Toronto's gay village is becoming increasingly concerned about missing members of their community.

A Facebook group in Toronto called Missing Rainbow Community worked overtime in response to Andrew Kinsman's disappearance. A 49-year-old homosexual, he loved his work, volunteer positions, his friends, and his old cat. The Facebook group, which had 600 members at the time, began tying other missing men to Kinsman. Kinsman's friend, Greg Downer, was at the center of the community effort.

The number of missing men who may be connected began at age 12, but the final total after receiving the information was 5.

Majeed Kayhan, Skandaraj Navaratnam, Abdulbasir Faizi, Selim Esen, Andrew Kinsman.

At the end of July 2017, the Toronto Police formed a new task force, Project Prism. They were to investigate the disappearances of Kinsman and Esen, looking for a link between the two men and the disappearances investigated under Project Houston.

Project Prism was overseen by Investigator Michael Richmond of Sargent and led by Investigator Han Quiddinger (pictured), a 31-year veteran of the murder team. The project was rolled up by a sex crime officer and six officers from 51 divisions, three of whom were members of Project Houston.

The victim's lifestyle quickly hampered the investigation. Use dating apps and meet often with people you've never met.

Understanding this issue, Downer says direct dating apps will face many difficulties for police to obtain judicial approval for collecting data from popular dating app servers located outside of Canada. -I requested them to provide the user with an option, and I agree that their data will be released to the police if they go missing. A safety hotline has also been set up for those who are reluctant to speak to the police.

DS Idsinga allegedly stated that "significant evidence" was collected in late July relating to Kinsman, as his disappearance was reported within 72 hours. It remains unclear what this evidence is.

Over the months of August and September, police received manufacturing orders mandating the release of data from Google, Rogers, Bell, Telus, Royal Bank and Manulifebank. Later, vehicle and phone tracking warrants were obtained.

During this time, Bruce MacArthur was formally identified as a suspect, according to an edited warrant and police document partially released by a judge in mid-2018. At the request of September 8, McArthur was named when Project Prism demanded a warrant judicial seal. And the subsequent request to seal all warrants issued between September and November referred to "Investigation at Bruce MacArthur."

In October, more information was granted to Yahoo, Air Canada, additional banks, and LGBT publisher Pink Triangle Press.

"I can't help but wondering if Bruce MacArthur said it. This makes my life easier because these are the people who no one cares to pay attention to."-Vijayanathan

On October 3, plainclothes police officers arrived at Dom's auto parts in Courtes, Ontario, 70 kilometers northeast of Toronto. They were looking for

MacArthur's 2004 Dodge Caravan. Dominic Vetere, the owner of Dom's Auto Parts, confirmed that he bought the van on September 16th.

Vans were towed and police also filmed a copy of a store surveillance video showing MacArthur visiting the store. Better later said police said to him that he had found a minute amount of blood in the car.

On December 4, Project Prism was granted a general warrant for MacArthur's apartment. According to sources, police secretly infiltrated MacArthur's apartment and cloned his computer's hard drive. It was exactly the next day that Project Prism warned the gay community to look out for dating apps.

At a press conference scheduled for December 8, Project Prism investigators elaborated on the progress. However, despite their search, they said they had no evidence of the disappearance of five men, utilizing resources from dog units and drones.

But just one month later, after working for 15 hours without a break, the break occurred even after completing a 72-hour thorough investigation. Shortly thereafter, on January 17, two pieces of evidence were revealed that directly linked the disappearances of MacArthur, Kinsman, and Esen. Immediately 24-hour surveillance was begun on MacArthur and instructed to immediately arrest if MacArthur was observed to be "alone".

Just one day later, a young man entered the MacArthur Thorncliff Park apartment.

Arrest
Believing that the life of the young man was at risk, police officers attacked MacArthur's apartment and arrested him. Internally, sources close to the survey revealed that the young man was tied to bed. He was scared but he was not injured.

Based on blood evidence found in the confiscated van, police came to arrest MacArthur, armed with multiple extensive search warrants. The evidence found in MacArthur's apartment prompted investigators to prosecute MacArthur. Their bodies were not found, but DS Idsinga said police had a "pretty good idea" of how they died. He also said he was pleased with the lack of a corpse, but in the end enough evidence to confirm the conviction of the murder.

Sources close to the survey said a photo of the alleged victim was found in a search of MacArthur's dwelling, which led to such prompt charges. Sources have been quoted by several media outlets and pictures and photos of the dead MacArthur victims have been found on his computer.

He kept the pictures as a trophy.

While a warrant was executed to search MacArthur's residence, five other warrants were executed to search for properties related to MacArthur's landscaping operations. The Maddock House and one of the Toronto Houses were owned by Roger Hollan, a friend of the landscaped MacArthur family. Another property searched belonged to MacArthur's once long boyfriend. These three properties were released to their owners a week later.

Of greater concern to investigators was the 53 Mallory Crescent in the Toronto area of Leaside.

The homeowner has agreed with MacArthur. He will take care of their garden in exchange for storage space in their garage.

Forensics
Leaside homeowners were banned from their homes that day, allowing investigators to do a thorough search of the land dating back to the canyon. In a search assisted by corpse dogs and members of a severe urban search and rescue team, two large planter boxes were wrapped and removed.

Police announced on January 29 that they had found at least three skeletal remains in the confiscated planter's box. Although the body has not been identified yet, investigators say that MacArthur's three-time murder was due to Project Houston's subject matter, Majeed Kaihan, Soroushmamudi disappeared in 2015, and Dean's presumed death. I felt there was enough evidence to add the count, Risowick, a homeless man who had never been reported missing.

It was at this time that DS Idsinga confirmed that DS Idsinga was treating the investigation as a serial murderer's investigation of the evidence hidden in the city. The incident is "unprecedented", involving hundreds of police officers and investigating 30 properties. Mark Mendelson said the investigation "was done in Toronto, the largest ever," as the Ontario police, state forensic services, and forensic center helped the investigation and were former murder agents.

Criminologist Western University professor Michael Arndfield said the method of disposing of his victims suggested a sophisticated serial killer who developed his technique over time. And since most serial murderers start murdering in their twenties, we shouldn't be surprised if the MacArthur crime dates back decades.

If this were true, it would make MacArthur anywhere in the world the longest running serial killer on record. (We are #1! We are #1!)

On February 8, investigators announced they had found three more bodies in more planters at Leside House. One of these three was identified by fingerprint as Andrew Kinsman.

Additional planter boxes have been confiscated from throughout the city and other homes have seen forensic existence. The Leside home became a "zero ground" for police and forensic investigators who set up a command post at the property and spent nearly a month investigating the area. Bring heaters into the tent to fight the frozen ground and complete the excavation of the two sewer lines. On February 11, the house and property survey was completed and released to the owner. The owner asked the police to leave a tape of the crime scene to deter an increasingly harassing reporter.

On February 23, a single murder case was filed against MacArthur for the sixth time after dentistry records identified the remains of Scandala Navaratnam, another subject of the Project Houston Task Force. Mahmudhi's body was also decisively identified at this point. Both sets of corpses were found in Leighside's house planters.

After exhausting all the options to identify a series of relics found in planter boxes, police announced a "modified" photo of a man who died hoping the public could help. Held an unprecedented press conference. Police received more than 500 tips on the photos, 22 of which were found to be reliable and needed further investigation. At this press conference, they also announced that the seventh body was recovered from the Leaside planter.

A month later, MacArthur was charged with the 7th 1st murder of Abdul

Basil Faizy's death. On this charge, MacArthur is now officially official with the deaths of all three from a survey in Project Houston, and the other two (Kinsman and Esen) who rounded five men connected by members of the Facebook group. Indicted, Missing Rainbow Community in Toronto.

"The community has already created the link before police do it," says Vijayanathan. "At least in a more public way."

MacArthur has now been charged with the death of all six identified bodies, and the death of Majeed Kaihan, whose body has not yet been discovered. And police still left the body of an unidentified man, but had not charged him without revealing his identity.

This was changed on April 11, and MacArthur was charged with one-eighth of the 1st-degree murder of the death of Kirshankham Kanagaratnam, which police released for help. However, police confirmed that his identity was not confirmed by any of the hints generated, but with the help of private international agencies said it was confirmed. Kanagaratnam was Tamil's asylum-seeker under a deportation order. He was never reported missing. Last contact with his family was in August 2015, and police believe he was someday killed between September 3 and December 14 of the year.

In collaboration with forensic investigations at facilities around Toronto, we spent hundreds of hours all over MacArthur's apartments. They moved from room to room. In other words, it took me several weeks to touch the bedroom. The investigation finally ended on May 11, after spending about four months and the time of ten forensic officers. Over 18,000 photos were taken and over 1800 items were collected.

DS Idsinga said he needed an exhaustive level of performance, as he believed the first murder was done eight years ago.

The investigation of Leside's home and MacArthur's apartment holds records of the largest forensic investigations ever conducted by the Toronto Police.

Cold case
Police have worked with other Canadian forces and international forces since February 2018, with the understanding that MacArthur's crimes can be traced back decades, with hundreds of unsolved murders. We have started

investigating the occurrence of a missing person and sudden death.

Police have begun to receive tips from around the world, including in the countries where MacArthur is on vacation.

DS Idsinga said the investigation would take years to complete.

Police sources knew that MacArthur was using a payphone instead of a cellphone, avoiding the location of surveillance cameras and carefully covering his trucks everywhere he went. I was told that I was said to have been. According to sources, police say MacArthur liked to target vulnerable men who have unfixed addresses or hide their homosexuality from friends and family.

DS Stacy Garrant of Toronto's Cold Case Unit said it actively compiles a list of cases that may be related to MacArthur, while active cases take precedence over older cases. It was. So far, there is a list of 15 murder cases related to gay villages, which so far fit the general profile of the suspected victim, and was prepared for further investigation. It was

The cold incident involved a series of brutal murderers of gay men in the village from 1975 to 1978, MacArthur was 23-26 years old, working only a few blocks south of the village. . Victims of these particular cases, all homosexuals, were found at home, nakedly tied to bed, and stabbed or beaten to death in a process known as "overkilling."

The plan was to allow corpse dogs to work more accurately by returning to the other 30 MacArthur-related facilities after the ground had melted. DS Idsigna said he was interested in finding excavations at three specific facilities, including a revisit of Leaside's home. Influx of hints has increased the potential searchable properties from 75 to 100 (including outside cities).

The search started by the second week of May and ended by mid-June. Police then narrowed down the list to identify areas that needed further searches.

One of those places was a forest canyon behind the Leaside property. Between 4th and 13th July, with the help of a dog team and a forensic anthropologist, 20 investigators sifted through a pile of compost and dug up the ground.

all. single. Day. As a result of this new survey, more human remains have been collected.

On July 20, it was announced that the body was confirmed to be from Kaihan. MacArthur had already been charged with his murder charges, but his body had never been found.

"I'm really happy to know that Majid and his family can take a break and the community can take a break," the organization reports on some of their missing gay men from South Asia. Haran Vijayanathan asked for a review of how they handled the years leading up to the arrest of MacArthur.

Idsinga said the police did not find evidence that MacArthur was associated with other deaths after the investigation, but the investigation into the cold case will continue.

"To the best of our knowledge, the first murder took place in 2010," Idsinga told reporters. "We have eight victims identified and hope only eight."

Waterloo Local Police contacted the Ontario Predatory Crime Investigation Coordinator to inquire about MacArthur in November 2002 in connection with the disappearance of David McDermott from Kitchener. John Riley of Meaford, Ontario may also be a victim. He went to Toronto to find a landscaping job, planned to stay in a village shelter, and disappeared in May 2013.

Looking for more information on cold cases, The National Post did an interesting study of 186 Toronto cold cases and looked for patterns.

Legal procedure
In January 2018, all court proceedings involving MacArthur were banned from publishing, limiting the information available in the media.

The judicial preliminary hearing was scheduled for June 20. It was a private meeting with the King, defense lawyer, and judge, but it is believed that the issue addressed was to resolve the case without trial – McArthur on guilty plea. At the moment this is not happening.

Given the amount of evidence that needs to be cataloged and disclosed, some fear that the trial will be years away. However, a recent Canadian Supreme Court ruling has set new rules that require defendants to complete their trials within 30 months of being charged, except in exceptional circumstances.

Is the amount of evidence considered an exceptional situation?

Currently, MacArthur is detained, quarantined, and constantly monitored for suicide in the Toronto South Detention Center.

That's all for the time being! News has not been news since July. This is both good and bad. MacArthur currently has no plans to appear in court. At this point, I'm just waiting for a trial. And what the challenges will be!

Whenever that happens, you can be sure I'm following it and writing about it here.

Now that you have become an expert in the Bruce MacArthur case, watch comedy and play with your puppies as a palette cleanser. To be honest, this can be very tiring mentally.

27 THE COLD CASE OF APRIL TINSLEY

Eight-year-old April Tinsley was abducted the morning of Good Friday 1988 when she picked up an umbrella and returned home from her friend's house.

By 3 pm, April mother Janet Tinsley had reported that her daughter was missing. The investigation was immediately conducted by the police, but was found almost empty-handed for two days. One witness reported that he was driving in a light blue pick-up truck, dragging the April into the truck and seeing him away from the car.

On the third day, Jogger discovers the body of a girl in a ditch on DeKalb County Road 68 near Spencerville. Indiana Police and DeKalb County Sheriff's Office arrived on the scene. They found one of the girl's shoes, about 1,000 feet west of the body.

Janet and Michael Tinsley identified the body as late April and conducted an autopsy.

An autopsy revealed that April died of suffocation and was raped. During the forensic investigation, the investigators learned that the murderer, a stranger, had left her DNA in her girl's underwear.

Despite the eyewitness testimony and DNA of the man on the truck being left behind, there were no arrests and the case began to cool off.

Two years later, on May 21, 1990, police were called into the barns on Schwartz Road and Indiana 37. There words were written out on the barn door, and it appeared that the murderer acknowledged the killings in Tinsley. "I kill April Marie Tinsley, eight. I'll kill Haha again."

Still, this memo did not provide a new lead.

Then, in the spring of 2004, 16 years after his death in April, police were dispatched to four different locations around Fort Wayne, based on information that the killer left a note inside the mailbox and on the girl's bicycle handlebar. It was. At each location, police found a zip-lock bag with handwritten notes on yellow lined paper and used condoms and polaroid photos to partially show the male body and masturbate him. It was

Read one similar note, grammatical error, or misspelled note, like the one found at the barn door 14 years ago. If you haven't reported this to the police, my next victim is AN I can't read this on paper [tomorrow] or local news or I [will] blow [not see this on]. "

The DNA profile was developed on the basis of samples found in used condoms and announced that "it was determined to match the profile developed from April M Tinsley underwear." Despite this new provocation from the killer, no arrests were made.

In April, family and friends celebrated the 30th anniversary of Tinsley's death. Members of the FWPD attended and assured everyone that they would continue to work to resolve the cold case.

In May 2018, Detective Brian Martin with Fort Wayne Police enabled its warranty and arranged for DNA testing and analysis at Parabon Nano Labs using stored evidence samples. On July 2, 2018, the institute was able to narrow down the DNA sample to two living siblings. This connection was created using a published genealogy database study by the well-known genealogist CeCe Moore. Moore's study has also led to the arrest of a man in Washington in a double murder in 1987. The use of the same database by researchers is also responsible for guiding police to arrest a man in a series of killings caused by the Golden State Killer.

In this case, the match caused the investigators to zero the investigation of one of his brothers, John D. Miller (59). Fort Wayne and Indiana police have placed Miller under surveillance at his mobile home at Block 13700 on Main Street in Graville.

On July 6, police secretly collected garbage from Miller's residence, looking specifically for items containing his DNA. In the litter pile, investigators found three used condoms. The condom was sent to the Indiana Police

Institute for DNA testing. And within three days, the test lab contacted me that the DNA profile extracted from the condom in the Millers trash bin matched the DNA profile of the condom found in 2004 and the DNA found in Tinsley underwear. ..

Yesterday, July 15, detectives Brian Martin and Clint Hetrick approached Miller at home and asked the police to talk. The detectives then asked, "Do you have any idea why we want to talk to you?" Miller replied, "April Tinsley."

During an interview with Miller, Miller first said, "I can't," when asked to explain exactly what happened in April Tinsley. But after a while, he relaxed and confessed to Tinsley's abduction and murder.

He took her while she walked along Hoagland Avenue and brought her back to his mobile home where he raped and choked her to prevent her from being reported to the police. Said. He told police, "It took 10 minutes for her to die." After Tinsley died, Miller told police again that he had raped her body, and in the morning he put her body into his car, up to DeKalb County Road 68 where he threw her body into a ditch. I drove.

The next day, when the news didn't show any reports of the incident, Miller said she drove her body to make sure it was still there. At this time, he found one of his shoes in the car and threw them through the window while driving.

The following news release was sent to local media on Sunday at approximately 1pm.

Fort Wayne Police and Indiana Police Investigators Arrested John D. Miller (M/W, DOB) on Morning of July 15, 2018: In Graville, Indiana, Related to April 1 Murder Case On July 7, 1959, Miller was preliminarily charged with murder, child abuse, and imprisonment. He will appear in his first court tomorrow at the Allen High Court at the Buddy Meek Justice Center for the first hearing. If a possible cause is found, the state of Indiana will be given 72 hours to file a formal complaint.

An affidavit of possible causes is included in this press release. In accordance with the Indiana Code of Professional Conduct for Lawyers, no more factual information will be published. As the event unfolds, additional information regarding court dates will be released from this office.

The investigation is underway by Fort Wayne Police and Indiana State Police with the support of the Federal Bureau of Investigation and the Allen County Sheriff. Similarly, prosecutors' offices in Allen and DeKalb counties.

A press conference will be held at 11:00 am on Tuesday, July 17th. The Omni Room is located on the second floor of the Police Operations Center at Rousseau Center, one of the main streets of Fort Wayne, Indiana. No additional information will be disclosed until the press conference.

Miller was taken to Allen County Jail where he was detained on charges of murder, child abuse and imprisonment. He was supposed to appear in his first court yesterday.

On the same day Miller was arrested and ID Discover Channel aired a special broadcast in an unsolved case in April.

Based on the notes, provocations, and brief confession that Miller randomly left for years, I got the feeling that he wanted to be caught.

I object to the death penalty in principle, but I would uphold any amendments to the law that would apply the death penalty in the presence of solid evidence and confession. In this case, I would not object to the removal of John D. Miller from Earth. He's a perfectly good waste of oxygen.

28 THE YOGOURT SHOP MURDERS

Amy Ayers, 13, Eliza Thomas, 17, Sisters Sarah and Jennifer Harbison, 15 and 17 naked bodies of four girls were found naked, dressed in their own clothes, and headed after firefighters were dumped. It has been almost 27 years since I was shot. A "incredible yogurt!" shop that used hundreds of gallons of water to stop a arson suspected of arson.

The three girls were stacked on top of each other, badly burned and melting together. At least one girl was raped.

Detective John Jones said: "I saw the murder but not the four, and not all four were detained, four removed, or four burned. There is none."

The problem in this case is that it is not technically solved yet.

These are the facts: On December 6, 1991, Jennifer Harbison and Eliza Thomas were working in a late shift in the store. Jennifer's sister Sarah, and Sarah's friend Amy stopped by to wait for the girl while they closed the store for the night. They were planning an overnight stay.

At about midnight, a patrol Austin police officer noticed smoke from a yogurt shop and notified his dispatcher. After the firefighter extinguished the flame, he entered the store and found a corpse.

Investigator Jones investigated the case with his partner Mike Huckabay.

"Dark inside, lots of smoke, scorching insulation everywhere. Hackabay remembered in 48 hours. "In Vietnam, I didn't think'nothin' would be comparable. Well, this matches it We're in Austin, Texas, right under the street from where we live."

From the beginning, the problem with the incident was in the lack of evidence-destroyed by flames or by water that extinguishes flames. And forensic science in the early 90's is not today's science.

"If that happened today," Hackabay said, "perhaps there was a better way to handle the crime scene. But at that time we had the best possible scene we had. Processed."

Jones and Hackabay tracked down Satanists and serial killer. At that time he was in the Austin area.

"He said all over,'If I did that...I'm proud of it so I'll say it,'" Huckabay said.

Investigators opened the tipline to get the public's help, but what they faced was a dead end, despite a rush of dead end chips.

"It doesn't stop the phone from ringing. There was a stack and stack of chip sheets on the desk," Huckabay said.

At some point, police needed to check out 342 suspects based on what they knew. $500 and $40 were lost from the register. Two guns were used during the crime. The door was locked when the firefighter first tried to access the scene. The storage procedure was to lock the door 10 minutes before closing. Investigators have begun to focus on young teens, such as 16-year-old Maurice Pierce, who was arrested with a gun at North Cross Mall.

"He looked good. We had to move on top of him," Jones said. The investigators also picked up Pierce's friends, Michael Scott, Robert Springsteen, and Forest Wellborn, who were dating him on the day of the killing.

However, Pierce's gun trajectory did not match the gun used in the murder. "So we've reached the point where any of the four can't go any further," Jones said.

The high level of attention in the case also added a new element that criminals had to deal with: false confessions. Police admitted over 50 confessions, six of which were written and signed, and one of which was Mr McDuff, who admitted the killings on the 17 November 1998 execution. But the investigators have solid evidence.

"We weren't going to sign the line until we went beyond reasonable suspicion to reach certification standards," Jones said. "We felt like we owe our family to do it right."

Hucka Bay and Jones were removed from the incident and replaced by new investigators eight years later with no arrests or new prospects. In 1999, a new investigator arrested four suspects. In detention, Forest Wellborn, Michael Scott, Robert Springsteen, Maurice Earrings.

Today, they are all in their twenties, the same boys who were taken to Jones and Hucka Bay eight days after the killing and dismissed. I started to feel that the original two detectives were messed up. Michael Scott first confessed to the new detective.

Michael Scott: I remember seeing this girl. You hear the sound of a gun firing... Triggered only once. I hear another gun firing. I think you can hear a total of 5 shots.

Detective: Michael, you're doing well. tell me! Let's do this today! let's do it!

Michael Scott: I remember one girl screaming and terror.

Then Springsteen began telling the story and made a second confession to the new detectives.

Detective: You know you raped her. OK. Please speak.

Springsteen: I pierced my pussy with my dick and I raped her.

According to police theory, the four men, who were boys at the time, planned to rob the yogurt shop. Springsteen, Pierce, and Scott went into the store with guns, but Wellborn was waiting outside looking out. Something went wrong after the girl was tied up. Maybe Springsteen saw the opportunity to rape one of the girls and took it, perhaps they didn't want to leave a witness, but the murder began. And they burned the store to destroy the evidence.

Wellborn's involvement has always been suspicious. He remained innocent, vowed he wasn't a watchman, and he wasn't there. He also alleges that police tried to force false confessions from him. But he never cracked.

In a 48-hour interview, Wellborn said of the detective: They become honest with my face and tell me that everything I said was a lie. I didn't mean to lie about that. "

Despite arresting all four on murder charges, they were unable to file charges against Wellborn. They tried twice, and neither jury failed to indict. Eventually the charges against him were dropped. The charges against Maurice Pierce were also dropped. Police were convinced he was the mastermind of the entire incident, but they had no evidence to prove it.

Thanks to the confession, everything fell apart, except for the lawsuit against Springsteen and Scott. But still there was a problem-more assertions of coercion.

"I was beaten, beaten and beaten by cops," said Springsteen. "They wouldn't let me leave until they got what they wanted to hear... and basically, they broke me."

In May 2001, the Springteen trial began. At trial, he was married and worked in the stock room. Springsteen has always maintained his innocence and pointed out that his defense has no physical evidence linking him to crime-no DNA, no ballistics, no blood, no hair. But it is difficult to explain why he confessed. Ironically, this was the only reason he was ever charged.

"There are psychological aspects that I don't understand," he said.

Springsteen's lawyer was George Sawyer, a large Texas lawsuit. "They were going to get a confession from Robert Springsteen. Limit. Sawyer said in 2009. They isolated him, they went to work, you're going to confess." "Oh, you will confess," he confessed by God. "

The only thing that can hang up outside observers is that Springsteen's statement got some of the details right. For example, he showed Amy's body position and knew she was shot with a .380 handgun.

Sawyer rewrote the details of a review that had been on Austin's streets for 10 years. "They were known to virtually all the young children who were interested in the case. They were there on the night of the murder and on that night."

The former detective of this case, Jones, refers to the language used in the written statement that the information was provided by the investigators. "For example, I had a Zippo lighter and lit it. When it fired, I heard an accelerator cry." Accelerant was a multi-syllable word," Jones said. It was "And I think it was his first polysyllabic word... I think he heard it before, yeah. Who calls a light fluid a promoter? That's a cop story is."

Jones and his partner almost insulted that they were not consulted with the new suspect when they picked up the four suspects, especially when everything was fresh, shortly after Jones first spoke to the suspects. it was done.

"We accepted them, and we didn't get anything close to them, they were still boys at the time," Jones explained. "I didn't expect it, and it's still not. That means people of that age can retain that information."

Judges discussed for 13 hours. Springsteen was found guilty and eventually sentenced to death in Texas. Almost two years later, Michael Scott was finally put to trial. He was also found guilty and sentenced to life imprisonment in prison without the possibility of parole.

But in 2006, both the Springsteen and Scott convictions were overturned by the Texas Criminal Court of Appeals. Reason: Everyone has the right to defend the accused under the sixth amendment. But in the case of Springsteen and Scott, their confessions were used against each other and they were never allowed to cross-examine each other at their trial. Conclusion: Their constitutional rights have been violated.

They will need to go to trial again. And the district attorney decided to do just that.

The prosecution now hoped to strengthen the case with new, more reliable DNA tests that have evolved over the last decade. Springsteen said he raped one of the victims, but from the scene and new DNA results from the raped victim, Springsteen isn't a match, nor are the other three men accused of crime. It has been found.

"[We know that Springsteen didn't rape her], it can't be true, I know it's not scientifically certain," Sawyer said.

However, the prosecution still decided to try both men again. But after a few months' delay, the judge decided to release Robert Springsteen and Michael

Scott without bail. They will wait for the retrial as freemen.

On December 23, 2010, Austin police officer Frank Wilson and his rookie partner made a traffic stop for a vehicle being driven by Morris Pierce in the north of the city. After a short foot chase, Pierce wrestled with Wilson, then removed the knife from his belt and stabbed Wilson around his neck. Injured Wilson then pulled out his gun and shot Pierce.

To date, Springsteen and Scott are technically still awaiting reconsideration. Because investigators don't admit that they may have chased the wrong person. Their theory is that if DNA did not match these four boys, then there must have been them and a fifth person.

"It's absolutely ridiculous," said attorney Amber Farrelly to spend a lot of time in the lawsuit and prove who believed he really committed the murder of a yogurt shop. "Why haven't they mentioned the fifth man all the time? The boys have never mentioned the fifth man. The DA office has never mentioned the fifth man. There is no second man."

"It's very close to the highway, actually the two main highways, and the tracks," she explained to the yogurt shop. "If anyone wanted to get in and out of Dodge quickly, I could do that. It's certainly not something I can say is an opportunity crime, it's deliberate, and definitely planned. Thing."

She believes the murderers were in a yogurt store that night. And the policeman missed it.

"I know exactly who killed those four girls. I have his DNA profile," she said. "I know who it is. I just don't know his name."

Farrelly has compiled a timeline — a detailed description of everyone who came to the yogurt shop that night. She discovered that the police had neither identified nor spoken to.

"They explained and interviewed 52 people who were in the yogurt shop that day," she replied. "Some customers mention one man, or two men at the end."

These two mysterious guys were still in the store when they closed. The last two are except girls. They are described by eyewitnesses as thin-haired, dirty-haired blondes, about 5 feet 6 in length. From the late 20s to the early 30s, I am wearing a military fatigue coat. The other is said to be a larger man in an oversized black jacket. Witnesses say the two men were sitting at a table at 10:47 pm when the girls were closing the store.

"No, absolutely not," Farrely said. "There was an open bank bag under the cash register. I think the motive for the crime was evil. It wasn't a matter of money, just what those men did. By hurting those girls did."

Farrelly believes the mysterious DNA belongs to one of these two men. The problem is to identify them.

"I believe that someday we will find them. I'm probably the only person in this case, and I hope someday I'll actually be able to identify this person by name," she said. ..

Something about this incident gives me three serious atmospheres in Western Memphis. It feels like the new investigators ran four teenage men on the railroad at the time, as the family and the city wanted answers. The person to blame. The evidence that brought the investigators to their center is based on nothing.

In all of my investigations I found nothing to suggest that these four guys were in the yogurt shop on the day of the murder. It was because Pierce was arrested at the mall with a gun. And their time in jail is the result of their confession.

29 MARY BELL

Mary Florabel was born on May 26, 1957 in Northumberland, England, to a 17-year-old sex worker, Betty and a petty criminal, Billy Bell, who was not her real father. A family of three lived together in the White House. Road in the Scottswood area of Newcastle. The White House Road was just as there was always unemployment and police always present due to domestic violence issues, drug activity and sex workers.

Billy Bell protected most of Mary while Betty traveled north to work on Glasgow's more lucrative streets. Billy was eventually destined for prison for armed robbery, but was kind to Mary and loved her dearly.

This was in contrast to how Betty treated her young daughter. Reportedly, Betty consistently beat young Mary, and her young daughter abused Mary for sexual abuse, even passing her to her sex work client who paid Betty. The family later recalled in Bita's biography "Mary Bell's Incident" that Betta tried to kill Maria more than once to make her look like a coincidence. The family was always in suspicion when Mary "falled" through the window and "accidentally" consumed dangerous amounts of sleeping pills.

Mary's best friend on White House Road was 13-year-old Normabel (irrelevant). Both two young girls grew up in a violence and crime normalization environment. But even children who are accustomed to certain elements know that they are angry when they can't put them into words, missing what other children get. Norma regularly fought this anger into the playground with his fists and was known as a bully. The two young girls were connected through hatred and formed a dangerous team.

On May 25, 1968, the day before Mary Bell's 11th birthday, a group of boys were collecting trees in an abandoned house. At number 85, Martin Brown's body was found in his bedroom on the streets of St. Margaret. He was lying on his back, stretching his arms on the cross like Jesus, surrounded by rubble and debris, bleeding from his mouth.

Martin Brown was four years old.

An ambulance arrived at the scene and tried to revive Martin. Lacking physical evidence, signs of struggle, or visible damage to the body, investigators assumed Martin was involved in a tragic accident and did not investigate further.

The next day, an intrusion occurred in a Scottswood nursery. The nursery was destroyed and angry notes were written everywhere. They won't make sense to the police later. There was a warning in the memo. And confession: I will kill you as I come back.

9 weeks later: July 31, 1968. Brian Howe, 3 years old from White House Road, was last seen playing with his dog on the street. After dinner, his parents called him, but he didn't go home. The Howe family began a search for the neighborhood, but when Brian seemed to be really nowhere, they called the police. At night, police, neighbors, and the Howe family searched for infants.

Around 11 pm, Brian was found in a wasteland near his home, covered in a blanket of grass and weeds. Unlike Martin Brown, it was clear to police that Brian was the victim of the murder. There were bruise and wounds around his neck when he was strangled. A wound covered his face and blood driped from his mouth.

Chief of Officer James Dobson was in charge of investigating Brian Howe's death. He was also on the scene a few weeks ago when Martin Brown was found in an abandoned house on the street. He began to provide tentacles for suspected child abuse in the area.

Pathologists ruled that Brian Howe was strangled between 3:30 and 4:30 pm. He noticed pressure marks around the boy's neck and across his nose. Brian Howe was suffocating carefully and intentionally. Pathologists have discovered even more sinister things. His hair was cut, his legs were dissected, a 'M' was carved on his stomach, and his penis was cut.

Dobson determined that the cuts on the child's body were angry and claimed to be curious and playful.

"There was terrible playfulness about it, and terrible tenderness if you wanted," Dobson said. "And, for some reason, its playfulness made it not scary, but rather scarier."

On Brian Howe's funeral morning, Dobson attended to observe the crowd. And here he first suspected Mary Bell. He remembered that her actions were in the way, which fully convinced her of guilt.

"Mary Bell stood in front of Howes's house when the coffin was brought out. I was looking at her..." Dobson said. "And when I saw her there, I knew I wouldn't dare risk another day. She stood there laughing. Laughing at her hands and rubbing. I thought: My god, I have to take her, she will do another."

Dobson has decided to arrest Mary Bell and Norma that afternoon.

During their interrogation, the girl's remarks went through many changes, and police slowly chipped to find the truth. On August 4, Normabel broke up and revealed that what she vowed was the complete truth.

Norma told police that Mary would take her with him to show Brian's body. Police took her back to the spot where the little body was found and tested if she was telling all the truth. Norma landed on the ground and lay in the same location and location where Brian was found, convincing the police after she actually saw the infant. She also showed police who hid the scissors Mary used to cut the boy's body and genitals.

Police did not believe Norma's claim that she was not involved in the killing of Brian Howe. After associating the killing of Howe with the killing of Martin Brown, the two girls were charged with two manslaughter charges in August 1968.

During a nine-day trial, Mary appeared to be far from being accused. She wasn't bored, but managed to leave the space occupied by court lawyers, juries, and all other attendees. Still, she seemed alert at that moment, watching her movements around her with ethereal blue eyes. She obstructed all the adults who cared for her during the lawsuit, "giving them will."

Mary didn't understand what would happen if she was found guilty, but she knew what would happen to her if she was acquitted. Her mother beat her to death.

On December 17, 1968, Normabel was acquitted of her accusations, but Mary was convicted of manslaughter for lessening her liability, and the jury said she "showed classic symptoms." Leading from the court-appointed diagnosis of a psychiatrist mentioned. Of psychosis. "

Judge Cussack described her as dangerous, and she said, "we have run very seriously for other children." She was detained for the pleasure of Her Majesty's Majesty and sentenced to imprisonment for virtually unlimited time. She was initially sent to a secure unit in the Red Bank of Lancashire-25 years later, the same facility that houses one of James Burger's killer John Venables.

After her belief, Mary received great attention from the British press. Her mother, Betty, repeatedly sold stories about her to the media, often giving journalists sentences that she claimed to be her daughter. Mary herself was talked about when she temporarily escaped from a moorish court's open-air prison, which had been in custody since her move from a young criminal institution to an adult prison a year ago in September 1977. Her penalty for this was a 28-day loss of prison privileges. For a while, Bell also lived in a girl's villa at Cumberrow Lodge in South Norwood.

In 1980, at the age of 23, Mary was released from an open prison in Askham Grange after working for 12 years. She was given anonymity (including her new name) and she was able to start a new life. Four years later, she had a daughter who was born on Mary's birthday.

Mary's daughter was unaware of her mother's past until 1998, when the place was discovered by a reporter. Mary and her daughter had to leave the house with their bed sheets on their heads. Since then, they have been forced to move home several times until the court finally ordered in 2003 that Mary's daughter should also have a lifetime of anonymity. As a result, court orders that permanently protect the identity of British prisoners are sometimes referred to as the "Mary Bell Order."

In 2009, Bell was reported to have become a grandmother. Today, Mary Bell is 60 years old.

30 THE WEEPY-VOICED KILLER

Between 1980 and 1982, Paul Michael Stefani killed three women in the Minneapolis-St. Paul area.

He received the terrible nickname "The Weepy-Voiced Killer" (to be honest, I can't use that name). After he committed the murder, he anonymously called the police and reported the crime. I'm always uplifting and emotional and crying.

New Year's Eve 1980 – A 20-year-old student at Stevens Point University, Karen Potak walked home at around 1 am after a night out to celebrate his holiday with friends. Potuck was ambushed and beaten as she walked down the street, drunk, and finally intended to return home. Tired by the irons on the tires.

Around 3 am, police received a phone call from a man who wanted to report an assault. The caller's voice was full of emotions when the police announced the location of the crime scene. He said, "There is a hurt girl here." When a 911 operator asked for his name, Stefani hung up.

Police and paramedics rushed to the scene and found Potac sticking to life, even though her brain was exposed through a crushed skull. Potak was taken to the hospital and began to recover surprisingly physically, but she had no memory.

On June 3, 1981, a group of boys walked through a lush area near Interstate 35E. At the same time, Stefani was calling the police. He shouted. I just stabbed someone with an ice pick. do not stop. I will keep killing someone! "

Police managed to return the call to a payphone at the bar across from the bus stop, but when the call arrived, the caller was gone for a long time.

The boys finally found the body during the walk. The woman was finally identified as an 18-year-old Kimberly Compton. She was stabbed in the chest 61 times with an ice pick and then strangled with shoelaces.

Two days after Compton's body was discovered, police received another call from the murderer. He said he had no intention of killing Compton and would defeat himself. But he didn't. Instead, he called the police again a few days later to apologize for not surrendering. He said: "I try not to kill anyone else... I couldn't help it. I don't know why I stabbed her. I'm so angry about it. "

On July 21, 1982, Carol Kellogg arrived at the home of her 33-year-old friend Kathleen Green. The pair was scheduled to leave for a girl's vacation to Mackinac Island. Kellogg knocked on the front door, but had no answer. She put herself in, unlocked the door, greeted Greening, and searched each room she went to. There was a light in the bathroom, so she stopped and pushed the door open. She found greenery in the bathtub.

Greening's naked body was facing the water upwards, her head was under the faucet, and her knees were bent towards the front of the bathtub. The police judged the death to be an accident. Those who did not agree blamed Greening's estranged husband, but charges were never brought against him.

On August 5, 1982, 40-year-old nurse Barbara Simmons was in Hexagon Bar. She met the man and offered him a cigarette. He offered her a ride into the house. Simon's told the bartender that he took off with the man. She was discovered the next morning by a newspaper delivery walking along the Mississippi River. She was stabbed and died.

Once again, Stefani called the police. "Don't talk, listen... I'm sorry I killed that girl. I stabbed her 40 times. Kimberley Compton was St Paul's first overall."

Police began the investigation with the most obvious criminal – the Simons guy had left prison the night before. Witnesses were able to provide police with a male description: about 40 years old, 6 feet tall, 185 pounds, white, receding hairline.

Police tried to track down this mysterious man, but Stefani tried to find another victim. This time was Dennis Williams, a 19-year-old Minneapolis sex worker. On August 21, 1982, Williams worked as usual when Stefani approached her asking her for service. After discussing the price, Williams got into the car.

Once he got what he paid for, Stefani turned down the dead end. Williams got the odd feeling that something was wrong-this John hadn't returned to the area where he picked him up. Stefani attacked Williams with a driver and made a total of 15 strikes before deciding what to do. While she was being stabbed, Williams reached for a bottle near her feet, screamed, and smashed Stefani in her face with that bottle. Williams screamed and caught the attention of a man who lived nearby. He came to the aid of Williams, wrestled with Stefani and forced Stefani to escape from the scene.

Williams rescuers called an ambulance and were able to explain the attacker. While this was happening, Stefani was returning to his apartment. When he saw the damage the bottle had done to his head and face, he called 911 for help.

The 911 operator said that Stephanie was in a similar tone to the Weepy Voice Killer, with a facial injured man being sought after in connection with another crime just happening, the Williams stab. I noticed.

Police were dispatched to an apartment in Stefani where they were arrested and later charged with the second assault. Further investigation, thanks to the witnesses' explanations, also led to Stephanie's killing of Barbara Simmons.

During the trial, Stefani's ex-wife, sister, and ex-roommate all testified that the voice of the 911 call by the Weepee Voice Killer sounds like Stefani. But this was not enough to connect him to other murders suspected of being committed by the Weepy-Voiced Killer. Hysterical crying was argued to be too distorting for a completely positive ID.

In 1997, Stefani was diagnosed with cancer while serving 40 years in prison for the killing of Simon's and the assault of Williams. He was given less than a year to live. This news prompted him to confess his other murders. He claimed responsibility for Karen Potak, Kim Compton and Catherine Greening.

I had never called him later, so I had never been a suspect of Mr. Greening's death in a bathtub. know. In addition, the investigators found the name "Paul S" in Greening's address book, along with Stefani's phone number.

Overall, Stefani admitted that he attacked Karen Potak's assault, stabbed Kim Compton, drowned Catherine Green, stabbed Barbara Simons, and attacked Dennis Williams.

In 1998, a year after his confession, Stephanie died in Oak Parks Heights' largest safety prison.

31 THE WATCHER

In the summer of 2014, Derek and Maria Broaddas, in Westfield, NJ, bought their dream home for as high as $1.3 million. And it's damn gorgeous.

Built in 1905, behind a 10-year-old tree is a 3,920-square-foot single-family household with 6 bedrooms and 4 bathrooms.

But after the sold-out sign was posted, the neighbor noticed that the house was empty all summer. The new owners seemed too scared to move in. And after returning it to the market in February 2015, they soon found out that no one wanted to buy it from them.

They were stuck in this house. A house that someone claimed to be looking at. Not only did they look at the house, they were also interested in the children.

A mysterious stalker named "Watcher" forced Broaddas to flee his dreaming $1 million home for the safety of his children.

Three days after buying the property, the family received their first letter from the watcher.

"My grandfather saw a house in the 1920s, my father saw a house in the 1960s. It's my time now. I was watching and waiting for that second coming. The young blood I demanded made me a house. Do you need to meet? Once I know their name, I call them and draw to me."

In two more letters, he wrote:

"Do they still know what's on the wall? Over time. Now is my time. Why are you here? Find; they have it to show off it So they pay a price..."

"I'm glad to know your name and the name of the young blood you brought to me. Will the young blood play underground? Who has the bedroom facing the street? You'll know right away...you know who's in which bedroom so you can plan."

"I'm a human? I'm a watcher, and I've been managing my [house] for a good portion of 20 years."

Perhaps they were erased as ill pranks, but then a letter arrived.

He wrote:

"You changed it and made it so gorgeous. It yells what happened in the past and when I was roaming the hall.... When I ran from room to room, there was rich I imagined a life with residents."

"Let the young blood play again, as I once did. Stop making changes and leave alone."

One year after buying the house, Broaddas filed a civil lawsuit against the original owner who sold the house, allegedly not "knowingly and purposefully" revealing the history of the house.

In a lawsuit, Broaddas lawyer Lee Levitt wrote, "The couple has been consumed daily by the stress, anxiety and fear of what the'watchers' do." The couple said they would never have bought a house if they knew about the keeper. They claim that the former owner received a letter from the watcher but never revealed it. The family, The Woods, has counterclaimed that the letters they received were not threatening and they were now defamed by Broaddas.

Westfield Police and the Union County Public Prosecutor's Office were investigating a chilling letter, and even the mayor had asked the town to say something if it knew anything about the watchman.

"Our police department conducted a thorough investigation based on the facts and available evidence," police said. "It's not appropriate to discuss the details of the investigation. We talked to the Union County Prosecutor's Office to make sure no stones were left behind."

To date, there have been no arrests in the Watcher case and civil cases have remained unresolved.

What do you guys think? Will you live there?

www.ingramcontent.com/pod-product-compliance
Lightning Source LLC
Chambersburg PA
CBHW020333160726
47992CB00004B/1825